1961*

The Inside Story of the
Maris-Mantle Home Run Chase

PHIL PEPE

TRIUMPH
B O O K S

Library of Congress Cataloging-in-Publication Data

Pepe, Phil.
  1961 : the inside story of the Maris-Mantle home run chase / by Phil Pepe.
    p. cm.
  Includes bibliographical references.
  ISBN 978-1-60078-390-6
  1. Maris, Roger, 1934–1985. 2. Mantle, Mickey, 1931–1995. 3. Home runs (Baseball)—United States—History. 4. Baseball—United States—History. 5. Baseball—Records—United States. 6. New York Yankees (Baseball team) I. Title.
  GV865.M34P47 2011
  796.3570973'09046—dc22

                                                                2010039340

This book is available in quantity at special discounts for your group or organization. For further information, contact:

Triumph Books
542 South Dearborn Street
Suite 750
Chicago, Illinois 60605
(312) 939-3330
Fax (312) 663-3557
www.triumphbooks.com

Printed in U.S.A.
ISBN: 978-1-60078-390-6
Design by Patricia Frey

Contents

ACKNOWLEDGEMENTS

FOR TWO IMPORTANT REASONS, I am indebted to Roger Maris, without whom this book obviously never would have happened.

One reason is his enormous ability that enabled him to challenge and surpass the most prestigious record in baseball history. His achievement allowed me, at the outset of my baseball writing career, to go along on a momentous and historic journey.

The other reason is the esteem for Maris among his peers that caused them to speak glowingly and eagerly about him as a baseball player and as a man. In particular, my thanks for sharing their recollections of Maris go to Joe Altobelli, Sen. Jim Bunning, Joe DeMaestri, Whitey Ford, Jack Reed, Bobby Richardson, Bill (Moose) Skowron, and Dick Williams. Also of enormous help were the insights into Maris the man and the ballplayer that I gathered over the years in my conversations with Mickey Mantle.

My thanks, too, to Jeff Idelson, president, and Craig Muder, director, communications, of the National Baseball Hall of Fame and Museum and to the estimable Jack O'Connell, secretary-treasurer of the Baseball Writers' Association of America, who provided information regarding recognition of

Maris' feat in Cooperstown and details of his failure to gain sufficient votes for enshrinement in the Hall.

Finally, I would be remiss if I didn't single out Rob Wilson for conceiving the idea for this book. Thanks also to Tom Bast of Triumph Books for understanding the value in revisiting Maris' monumental achievement a half century after it occurred; to eagle-eye Ken Samuelson for his meticulous fact-checking; and to Noah Amstadter of Triumph, for his diligence in editing the manuscript and for his patience, enthusiasm, and encouragement.

INTRODUCTION

A HALF CENTURY AGO, Roger Maris mounted a serious challenge to Babe Ruth's exalted record for home runs in a single season, a record that had survived for 33 years. Several had challenged the record in those 33 years. A few had come close, but none—including the Babe himself—was able to topple the mighty Ruth's 1927 mark of 60 home runs in a single season. Consequently, most observers concluded that Ruth's record would never be broken.

In baseball's formative years, a home run was a rarity, an aberration, something thought to be a miracle or a mistake. Baseball was played in wide open fields that were not enclosed by fences, screens, walls, or grandstands, so home runs at the time were of the "inside-the-park" variety and treated more as a curiosity than something to be celebrated. In fact, the home run was scorned by the game's purists of the day who reasoned that the art of hitting was to, in the immortal words of "Wee" Willie Keeler, "hit 'em where they ain't," i.e., place the ball between fielders. There was, at the time, a greater priority on hitting the ball safely out of the reach of fielders than in hitting it great distances.

Three National Association players—Fred Treacey, a Brooklyn-born outfielder for the Chicago White Stockings;

Lipman (Lip) Pike, of the Troy Haymakers; and Levi Meyerle of the Philadelphia Athletics—shared baseball's first home run championship in 1871, each with four homers in a 28-game season. In 1879, the home run record was up to nine, and in 1883, Harry Stovey, playing for the Philadelphia Athletics of the American Association, increased the record to 14.

A year later, there was a proliferation of home runs in baseball. In one year, the number of home runs hit in the National League jumped from 124 to 321. The Chicago White Stockings, who had hit 13 home runs as a team in 1883, hit 142 a year later. Ned Williamson, who had hit only two home runs the previous season, set the baseball world on its ear and caused eyebrows to be raised when he blasted 27 home runs for the White Stockings in a 112-game schedule. Williamson hit 25 of his 27 homers at Chicago's tiny home park, where it was 180 feet down the left-field line, 300 feet to center, and 196 feet down the right-field line. The White Stockings hit 131 of their 142 home runs at home. A year later, balls hit over the left-field fence were ruled doubles. Chicago moved to a new, larger park the following season.

Williamson's record of 27 home runs in a season lasted for 34 years until a young man born in Baltimore came along. Playing for the Boston Red Sox, he turned the home run into an art form and, in the process, changed the game of baseball. His name was George Herman Ruth, but everybody called him "Babe." He didn't start out hitting home runs right away. He was a pitcher of such promise that by the time he reached the age of 23, he had won 67 major league games (23 in 1916 and 24 in

1917) and was considered the best left-handed pitcher in the American League.

The Red Sox were justifiably proud of their "Babe," but they didn't know what they had. He was their prized possession, and they viewed his future as a pitcher as one of limitless potential. At the same time, Ruth wielded a potent bat. In 1915, he led the team in home runs with four. In 1916, he tied for the team lead with three. Soon, it was clear that Ruth's longball hitting prowess could not be denied. In 1918, he divided his time among pitching (20 games), the outfield (59 games), and first base (13 games) and tied for the league lead in home runs with 11. By 1919, he was an outfielder who pitched occasionally, and he led the league in home runs with the awesome total of 29, which broke Ned Williamson's single-season record by two.

In 1920, his first year as a New York Yankee, Ruth raised the record to 54 and then to 59 in 1921 and to 60 in 1927. At the time, his home run total hardly caused a stir. It was widely assumed that the mighty Babe would eventually increase that record to 62, 65, even 70 home runs. He never did, topping out at 54 home runs in 1928.

In the three decades that followed, Ruth's record withstood equally serious challenges from three future Hall of Famers. In 1930, three years after Ruth had established his record of 60, Lewis Robert "Hack" Wilson of the Chicago Cubs blasted 56 home runs. Two years later, Jimmie Foxx of the Philadelphia Athletics—anointed as the heir to Ruth as baseball's premier power force—hit 58, a total matched six years later by Hank Greenberg of the Detroit Tigers.

In the 22 years following Greenberg's bid to surpass Ruth, Ralph Kiner's 54 home runs for the Pittsburgh Pirates in 1949 came closest to the record, adding to the belief that Ruth's record was forever.

*

But in 1961, along came Maris, taking dead aim at the record, threatening to topple Ruth as baseball's all-time single-season home run king, a threat that engendered regret, skepticism, fury, outrage, and even hate mail and death threats. Purists of the game, retired players, casual fans, baseball executives, and journalists expressed their dismay and disapproval that baseball's most enduring and most cherished record might be obliterated by so unworthy a mortal: a career .257 batter who had hit only 97 home runs in four major league seasons with a high of 39 the previous year.

Of all the players who could have been tapped to challenge baseball's most cherished, most legendary, and most revered record, Roger Maris was among the least likely. He never sought the spotlight, didn't want it, and didn't know how to handle it when he got it.

Maris was a simple man of simple tastes and a simple lifestyle. He was a devoted family man, not a flamboyant man about town; a private person, not a headline-seeking celebrity; a baseball player, not a god.

In many ways, chasing Babe Ruth's exalted record chipped away at Maris' popularity rather than enhanced it. To many, he was unworthy to stand alongside the great Babe—an ingrate, an upstart, a pretender to the great man's throne. Ruth, and the record, would have been better served had its most serious challenge come from Maris' teammate

Mickey Mantle, or Willie Mays, or Ted Williams, or Henry Aaron. But Roger Maris, of all people?

Who knows why the fates put their hands on the shoulders of Roger Maris, why the gods of baseball made him the chosen one? All we know for certain is that in 1961, 34 years after Ruth established the "unbeatable" record for home runs in a single season with 60, the shoulder of Roger Eugene Maris, born in Hibbing, Minnesota, and raised in Grand Forks and Fargo, North Dakota, was tapped and the chase was on, for better or for worse. In most cases, for worse.

Old-time baseball players, fans, and veteran journalists seeking to preserve and protect Ruth's record and his legend searched diligently for reasons to perpetuate Babe's legacy. Among those on the mission was the commissioner, Ford C. Frick, a former sportswriter himself and a close friend and occasional ghostwriter for the Babe.

Even a liberal, fair-minded, and progressive thinker like Chicago White Sox owner Bill Veeck had his misgivings about the challenge to Ruth's single-season home run record.

"It's the only record I don't want to see broken," Veeck said.

Expansion had come to baseball in 1961, the American League jumping the gun on the older, more established National League (it would follow a year later) by swelling from eight teams to 10 with the addition of two new teams, the Los Angeles Angels and the Washington Senators, formed to replace the team of the same name that relocated from the nation's capital to become the Minnesota Twins.

To maintain a balanced schedule—each team would play an equal number of games at home and away against each of the other nine—the number of games played in a season was increased from 154 to 162, thereby giving Maris—or any other player—an additional eight games in which to take aim at a record. Expansion also meant that American League hitters would have the opportunity to bat against an additional 20 to 25 pitchers who would previously have been playing in the minor leagues.

It was an unfair advantage for hitters, the traditionalists and self-appointed guardians of Ruth's legacy argued, and it had to be addressed.

✳

Into this swirling maelstrom of controversy, anticipation, and frenzy, I was suddenly, surprisingly, and naively dropped—grossly inexperienced and unprepared for what was to come and yet exhilarated by the opportunity to fulfill my life's dream: to write about baseball for a major metropolitan daily newspaper.

I had been consumed with the game as a boy growing up in Brooklyn and adopted the Dodgers as my team, the object of my passion and undying affection. I learned about baseball by listening to the syrupy sweet vocal intonations of Red Barber, the Dodgers' announcer, and honed my knowledge of the game and my love for the Dodgers with the help of aunts and uncles and cousins (no one in my immediate family had yet been bitten by the bug).

My aunt and uncle and cousins took me to my first major league game at Ebbets Field on Friday, May 8, 1942. I was seven years old and I remember thinking that the home team uniforms were the whitest white and the grass field was the greenest green I had ever seen. The Dodgers were playing the New York Giants (who were the Dodgers' archrivals, so, naturally, they became my archrivals, too) in a twilight game. The stadium was filled to overflowing (recent research told me the official attendance was 42,822, some 7,000 beyond the listed capacity).

The starting pitchers were Whitlow Wyatt for the Dodgers and Cliff Melton for the Giants. To my delight, the Dodgers won the game 7–6, and although much of how they did it has long since faded from memory, one thing has stayed with me all these years. The Dodgers scored the eventual winning run in the bottom of the seventh inning on a home run by Dolph Camilli, who had led the National League in home runs the previous season with 34 and would end up the 1942 season with 26 homers, tied with Johnny Mize for second in the league to the Giants' Mel Ott. Home runs were not plentiful in those days, so they were events to be celebrated. Camilli became an instant hero to this seven-year-old boy because of his home run bat.

Now I was trapped, hooked on baseball and the Dodgers like the most hopeless of addicts and destined to experience moments of great joy and greater despair.

I watched Jackie Robinson come to Brooklyn and help the Dodgers win the pennant in 1947 and 1949 but lose both times to the Yankees.

I watched the Dodgers lose the pennant to the Philadelphia Phillies on the final day of the 1950 season, and I saw the Giants' Bobby Thomson stick a knife in my heart with a home run against Ralph Branca in 1951.

I watched Johnny Podres beat the Yankees in the seventh game of the 1955 World Series and give Brooklyn its first baseball world championship. The next year I watched Don Larsen frustrate the Dodgers, and me, with the only no-hitter in World Series history, a perfect game no less.

In high school, I fed my love for the game by following my school's varsity team. I saw, and cheered for, Ken Aspromonte, and later his brother Bob, playing shortstop, a left-handed pitcher named Fred Wilpon, and a tall left-handed-throwing, right-handed-hitting first baseman named Sandy Koufax.

All the while, I kept dreaming the dream—that one day I would cover the Dodgers for a New York newspaper. It never happened.

After serving an apprenticeship working part time while going to college, I joined the sports staff of the *New York World-Telegram and Sun* to cover high school sports in April 1957, which would turn out to be the Dodgers' final year in Brooklyn.

When the Dodgers left, many of my friends switched their allegiances to the Yankees. I couldn't. It would have been tantamount to treason. Other friends gave up on baseball altogether. I couldn't do that either. My passion for the game was too deeply rooted. Besides, I was now a newspaper professional and I had the paycheck to prove it. I had to maintain my objectivity and hope that the time would come when I would cover baseball, even if it was the Yankees.

My time came midway through the 1961 season. A callow youth of 26, I had covered only a handful of major league games for the *New York World-Telegram and Sun,* several of them in the first part of that season. At midseason, through a series of unexpected and unfortunate circumstances that left my paper undermanned, I was assigned to take over as beat writer of the New York Yankees.

Wide-eyed and awestruck by the enormity of this assignment yet excited by the prospect of being a witness to and a chronicler of baseball history for posterity, I joined the fray and found myself covering and traveling with and even occasionally socializing with these men who had so often made my young, Dodgers-loving life so miserable—Yogi Berra, Whitey Ford, and Mickey Mantle in particular.

At the time, the pursuit of Ruth's home run record was a two-pronged challenge by teammates Maris and Mantle—newspaper headline writers had dubbed this dynamic duo "the M&M Boys"—and I was given one mandate by my sports editor: to write about Mantle and Maris every day regardless of whether they hit a home run or struck out four times.

I was determined to overlook my handicap of having missed the first half of the season, of not being privy to knowledge and information about the two principals I was charged with covering. I fretted that I was not invited into their inner sanctum, yet consoled by the thought that neither were my contemporaries and competitors.

I brought to the assignment no prior relationship with or partiality for either player, no preconceived notion about them, and no preference for either man. I remember thinking that Mantle was, with prejudice, the logical, more deserving, and understandably favored choice to break the record because of an often-spectacular, decade-long history as a Yankee (Maris had joined the team the previous year).

Mantle was the fourth in an unbroken four-decade line of Yankees superstars, following Ruth, Lou Gehrig, and Joe

DiMaggio. Five years earlier, he had become the 10th, and last, player in the major leagues to win the Triple Crown in hitting, leading his league, and the major leagues, in batting with an average of .353, in RBIs with 130, and in home runs with 52. Four times he had led the American League in home runs, and he had amassed a total of 320 homers. He was a popular figure in New York and a sympathetic figure because of a series of injuries that kept him from reaching even greater heights.

However, despite Mantle's résumé, I vowed to maintain my objectivity during the race for the record. I reasoned that whichever player exceeded Ruth's mark would have earned it. And I was eager to be a witness to baseball history. It turned out to be what was then, and still is, a remarkable journey and a revered memory.

CHAPTER ONE

Fargo

ROGER MARIS NEVER ASPIRED TO BE A YANKEE. Although the Yankees had long admired him from afar and coveted him for his smooth and powerful left-handed batting stroke that they envisioned as a perfect weapon for Yankee Stadium's easily reachable right-field seats and for his strong throwing arm, his deft fielding ability, and his sprinter's speed, their affection was unrequited.

Maris had no secret longing to play for baseball's wealthiest, most prestigious, and most successful team. He had no desire to go to New York to work, much less to live. He was a small-town guy, a country kid who hated the big city, was overwhelmed by its size, and felt suffocated by its mass of humanity. He was at peace in Kansas City, content as the member of a small-market team, away from the mainstream and the glare of the spotlight. It suited his values and his lifestyle.

The trade that would change Maris' life and alter the course of baseball history was made on December 11, 1959, seven years before Marvin Miller arrived and a decade before Curt Flood challenged and defeated the reserve clause. If he could have, Maris would have refused the trade. But he couldn't. He had no options, no choice but to accept the trade. A fierce competitor, he was at least pleased that he would be going to a team that was a perennial contender. He knew the Yankees were Mickey Mantle's team, and that also pleased him. He had no wish to be top banana, preferring the role of second fiddle. Above all, Maris was determined that the trade would not compromise his ideals or his convictions.

When he arrived in New York, Maris was a curiosity in a crew cut hairdo and a rube's wardrobe. His penchant for wearing white buckskin shoes was demeaned and scorned. When a friend admonished him that New Yorkers don't wear white bucks, Maris' response was to find the nearest Thom McAn shoe store and buy two more pairs.

*

There was no cacophony of bells, no crash of cymbals, no blaring of trumpets when Roger Eugene Maris slipped quietly into the world on September 10, 1934, in Hibbing, Minnesota, a sprawling but sparsely populated town in St. Louis County, some 70 miles northwest of Duluth and the mouth of Lake Superior. In fact, Roger Eugene *Maris* never did come into the world; he was born Roger Eugene *Maras,* of Croatian ancestry. His grandfather had come to the United States in 1900 and settled in Hibbing when the town was in its infancy. Roger's father, Rudolph Maras, grew up in Hibbing, worked for the Great Northern

Railroad; met and married Connie Sturbitz; and sired two sons, Rudolph Jr., and 15 months later, Roger. It wasn't until he was playing professional baseball that Roger, irked that some of his teammates were calling him Mar-ass, began spelling his name *Maris*. Eventually, all other members of the family did likewise.

Founded in 1893 by Frank Hibbing, the town, situated on the Mesabi Iron Range, was known as "the Iron Capital of the world." Given its size, Hibbing has produced more than its fair share of celebrities. In addition to producing the man who dared to chase Ruth, Hibbing has been home to musician Gary Puckett; professional basketball players Kevin McHale and Dick Garmaker; Jeno Paulucci, founder of Jeno's Pizza; Vincent Bugliosi, the prosecutor of Charles Manson; Carl Wickman, the founder of Greyhound Lines; and wine entrepreneur Robert Mondavi.

Roger was five when the family moved some 200 miles west to Grand Forks, North Dakota, leaving Hibbing nine years before the arrival of a seven-year-old named Robert Zimmerman, who later would change his name to Bob Dylan. After a decade in Grand Forks, the Marases were on the move again, this time 60 miles south to Fargo, North Dakota, where Roger would gain recognition as an outstanding athlete in four sports: baseball, football, basketball, and track and field—as well as a reputation for single-mindedness that he would carry into his professional life.

Largely because of the climate, the area in and around Fargo is known more for football than baseball (the legendary Bronko Nagurski came from International Falls, Minnesota, about 250 miles northeast of Fargo), and it was in football that young Maris made his mark. He and his brother, Rudy, enrolled in Fargo High School, and Rudy had an outstanding football season in his sophomore year. The Maris brothers envisioned themselves a potent one-two running punch the following season. But when the coach replaced Rudy as a starting running back and demoted Roger to the junior varsity, the brothers came up with an alternative solution. They would transfer to Bishop Shanley, Fargo's Catholic high school.

At Shanley, Roger flourished in his junior year. In one game, he returned four kickoffs for touchdowns, a national high school record that still stands (small wonder the record survives; after someone has burned you by returning two kickoffs for touchdowns, why would you keep kicking to him?). He would lead the Deacons to an undefeated season, their first of eight North Dakota State Class A football championships in nine years and the start of what would grow into a 59-game winning streak.

Maris' exploits on the football field attracted more than 50 colleges, including the University of Oklahoma, at the time the No. 1 college team in the nation under the leadership of the legendary Bud Wilkinson. For many years a story—later proved to be apocryphal—was circulated that Maris arrived in Oklahoma by bus, found no one from the university there to greet him, and promptly got on the next bus heading back to Fargo.

In fact, Maris, who had taken an entrance exam at Oklahoma, apparently was uncomfortable with the college scene and declined all offers to play football in college. By this time, he was also attracting attention in baseball and caught the eye of several major league scouts, not an easy thing for a kid from Minnesota or North Dakota where the high school baseball season often ends before the thaw sets in. Fortunately, there was American Legion baseball in the summer, and Maris' reputation as a hitter was growing enough for him to receive an invitation to work out for the Chicago Cubs in Wrigley Field. Apparently, Maris failed to impress any of the Cubs scouts, coaches, or manager Phil Cavarretta, because he left Chicago without a contract or so much as a "we'll keep our eye on you."

The Cubs' loss would prove to be the Cleveland Indians' gain. Area scout Jack O'Connor had been closely monitoring young Maris but assumed he'd be going to college to play football. When he learned that Roger had left the University of Oklahoma campus without making a commitment to the Sooners, O'Connor informed the Indians' chief scout, Cy Slapnicka, who was on a scouting trip in Chicago. Slapnicka had gained lasting fame as a judge of talent by discovering on a farm in Van Meter, Iowa, a 16-year-old right-handed fireballer named Robert William Andrew Feller, who would go on to win 266 major league games, strike out 2,581 batters, pitch three no-hitters and 12 one-hitters, and be inducted in the Hall of Fame.

When he received O'Connor's telephone call and heard the scout's glowing report about this kid from Fargo, Slapnicka left Chicago and flew to North Dakota to meet with Maris and his father. The scout told the elder Maris that the Indians were interested in signing his son, but first Maris would have to accompany Slapnicka to Cleveland where Roger would work out for the Indians' general manager.

It is one of life's coincidences that the general manager of the Cleveland Indians at the time was none other than

Hank Greenberg, who knew better than any man alive what it was like to challenge the mighty Babe Ruth's record for home runs in a single season. In 1938, 11 years after Ruth established the record by hitting 60 home runs, Greenberg, playing for the Detroit Tigers, made a serious bid to replace Ruth in the record books. With four games remaining, he had 58 home runs and seemed likely to hit the three home runs in four games he needed to replace Ruth as baseball's single season home run king.

But Greenberg failed to hit another home run in his final four games, the last three, coincidentally, played in Cleveland's cavernous Municipal Stadium. Now, 15 years later, here was Greenberg, general manager of the Indians, in that same stadium working out an 18-year-old prospect from Fargo, North Dakota, named Roger Maris.

Greenberg watched Maris, a left-handed hitter, pull the ball with power to right field. He watched him run down fly balls in the outfield, run the bases skillfully, and throw with velocity and accuracy. He liked what he saw, and he made Maris an offer, a $9,000 bonus to sign with the Indians. His stubborn streak surfacing once more, Maris refused.

They talked some more, they haggled, they negotiated, and Greenberg raised the ante to $15,000. Maris accepted. His football days were over. He was now a professional baseball player.

CHAPTER TWO

Moving Up

IT WAS NOT A COINCIDENCE that the Cleveland Indians' affiliate in the Class C Northern League was at Fargo-Moorhead, or that it was there that Roger Maris broke into professional baseball. Maris had done his homework. He knew the Indians had a farm team practically in his backyard, and he made it a condition of his signing that the Indians allow him to begin his career in his hometown, where he could live at home and play his first professional games in front of friends and family.

Young baseball players, especially those with no college experience, often find their first year as a professional a difficult adjustment. Loneliness and homesickness are common. Playing in his hometown, Maris experienced no such deprivation. He flourished in his first year even though at 18 (he wouldn't turn 19 until after the season) he was one of only four teenagers and the second-youngest player on the team. He batted an impressive .325 in 114 games, hit nine home runs, and drove in 80 runs.

At Fargo-Moorhead, the 18-year-old Maris roomed with Frank Gravino, a 30-year-old veteran who would hit 271 home runs in 12 minor league seasons but never make it to the major leagues. The highest Gravino reached on the minor league ladder was Rochester in the Class AAA International League for 116 games in 1948. Five years later, in Maris' first year as a professional, Gravino belted 52 home runs for the Fargo-Moorhead Twins. The following year, Gravino hit 56 home runs for Fargo-Moorhead and then hung up his spiked shoes.

While Gravino's baseball career was winding down, Maris' was on the rise. He was ready to move onward and upward, away from Fargo, up the ladder to Keokuk, Iowa, to play for the Keokuk Kernels in the Class B Three-Eye (for Illinois, Indiana, and Iowa) League.

It was at Keokuk that Maris first showed the long-ball power that would become his trademark a decade later. Under the patient and gentle tutelage of manager Jo-Jo White, who had played nine seasons in the major leagues with the Detroit Tigers, Philadelphia Athletics, and Cincinnati Reds and whom Maris would come to look upon as a surrogate father, Roger batted .315, 14th highest in the league; drove in 111 runs in 134 games; and led his team with 32 home runs, 11 more than the team runner-up. He was second in the league in homers, three behind the leader. His numbers caught the eye of the Indians' powers that be, and from that season on, Maris was on the fast track to Cleveland.

*

In 1955, the Indians sent Maris to Tulsa in the Class AA Texas League. It was his third season of professional baseball, he was just 20 years old, and he was being asked to leap-frog over Class A, a tall order, and play on a team that had 30-something teammates, such as Hank Schenz, Al Widmar, Jerry Fahr, Jay Heard, and George Schmees, all of whom had spent time in the big leagues and were hanging on either for the paycheck or in the hope of getting one more shot in the big show.

At Tulsa the famous Maris stubbornness surfaced once again, and he clashed with his manager, Dutch Meyer, a crusty old timer who had played in the majors with the Cubs, Tigers, and Indians. Meyer was livid when a throw from the outfield by Maris sailed over the cutoff man, over the third baseman, into the stands, and cost the Tulsa Oilers a game. He ordered the young outfielder to report early the next day to work on his throwing. Meyer stationed Maris in right field and hit him fly ball after fly ball, which Maris would catch and then throw to third base low enough for the ball to be handled by either the cutoff man or the third baseman.

When this went on for more than an hour, Maris simply walked off the field.

"Where the hell are you going?" asked Meyer.

"I'm through," Maris shouted. "I'm not blowing my arm out for you or anybody else."

"If you leave, you're gone," Meyer threatened.

But Roger Maris never did succumb to threats. He took off, perhaps out of frustration. At the time, Maris was struggling, batting .233 with one home run and nine RBIs in 25 games.

Meanwhile, Meyer had reported the incident to the Cleveland front office and demanded that the Indians remove the young outfielder from his Tulsa team. Maris returned home to Fargo, the Indians gave him a few days to cool off, and then ordered him to report to Reading in the Class A Eastern League, an assignment Maris welcomed, because the manager at Reading was his old baseball "father," Jo-Jo White.

They would become Yankees teammates six years later, but in 1955, Maris and Jack Reed were Eastern League rivals, Maris with Reading and Reed, a 22-year-old outfielder from Silver City, Mississippi, working his way up the ladder in the Yankees' farm system with the Binghamton Triplets, managed by former Yankees second baseman and 1945 American League batting champion George "Snuffy" Strinweiss.

Reed recalled, "Our best pitcher in Binghamton was Jim Coates, who could throw as hard as anybody." Nevertheless, Maris just feasted on Coates, according to Reed, "It looked like Maris just waited on Coates' fastball and he could hit it as good as anybody I saw, so I guess you can say I was impressed by Roger when I saw him in the minor leagues."

At Reading, Maris resumed his ascent in the Cleveland farm system, batting .289 with 19 homers and 78 RBIs in 113 games, which earned him an invitation to his first big-league camp with the Indians in Tucson, Arizona, in the spring of 1956.

*

In the 1950s, the Cleveland Indians were baseball's bridesmaids. They finished second in the American League for three straight years, 1951–53, as the New York Yankees concluded their record run of five consecutive World Series championships. The Indians interrupted that run with a record of their own in 1954, winning 111 games—at the time the most in American League history—and finishing eight games ahead of the Yankees. The Indians' record would last 44 years, until the Yankees won 114 games in 1998 (when the Indians won 111, they played a 154-game schedule; in 1998, the Yankees played a 162-game schedule. There was no asterisk to denote the increase in games, and none was so much as suggested).

The Indians finished second to the Yankees again in 1955, but it was becoming obvious that they were an aging ball team in need of reinforcements or a complete overhaul.

Their vaunted pitching staff, by now a little long in the tooth, was in a slow but steady decline. Bob Feller, the greatest pitcher of his time who, in four full seasons from 1939–41 and 1946, had won 102 games and struck out 1,115 batters—348 of them in 1946—and who was still a capable pitcher with 70 wins in the first five years of the decade of the 1950s, slipped to a record of 4–4 in 1955. He would fail to win a game in 1956 and retire after the season.

Hall of Famer Bob Lemon would win 20 games in 1956 at the age of 35, his seventh season of 20 victories or more, but it would prove to be a last hurrah. He would win only six more games and retire midway through the 1958 season.

Early Wynn, who would post his fourth 20-win season in 1956, dropped to 14–17 the following year and was traded to the White Sox that winter.

Mike Garcia, who, from 1951–54, had a record of 79–41, slipped to 38–39 over the next five years and was released after the 1959 season.

The two most productive hitters for the Indians in the early part of the 1950s were Larry Doby, a left-handed slugger, and Al Rosen, a right-handed basher. From 1950–55, they would combine to hit 341 home runs and drive in 1,229 runs.

The Indians had signed 23-year-old Doby out of the Negro National League, and he made his major league debut on July 5, 1947, 10 days short of three months after Jackie Robinson played his first game for the Brooklyn Dodgers and broke major league baseball's color line. A New Jersey native, Doby was the second African American in the major leagues and the first in the American League, subjected to as much prejudice, threats, loneliness, slurs, insults, and pressure as Robinson.

"The only difference," Doby would often say in later years, "[was] that Jackie Robinson got all the publicity."

A seven-time All-Star, Doby led the American League in home runs in 1952 and again in 1954 when he had his best year, leading the American League both in homers with 32 and RBIs with 126. It would be his last hurrah. When he fell off the following year to 26 homers and 75 RBIs, the Indians traded him to the Chicago White Sox for outfielder Jim Busby and shortstop Chico Carrasquel.

Rosen would drive in more than 100 runs in each of the first five seasons in the 1950s. In 1953, he led the American League in home runs with 43 and RBIs with 145 and was one base hit short of becoming the 10th Triple Crown winner in baseball history (he batted .3355 to the .3371 average of the batting champion, Mickey Vernon of the Washington Senators), and was voted the league's Most Valuable Player.

Beset by a series of debilitating injuries, Rosen fell off to a .244 average, 21 homers, and 81 RBIs in 1955 and a .267 average, 15 homers, and 61 RBIs in 1956. He retired after the season at the relatively young age of 32.

Spring training 1956 with the Indians would be Rosen's last, and he was a firsthand eyewitness to the changing of the guard. The Indians were excited about two young players who they believed would be worthy successors to Rosen and Doby, 21-year-old Roger Maris, a left-handed hitter like Doby, and Rocky Colavito, 22, and like Rosen, a right-handed slugger.

Maris impressed the veteran Rosen with his power, his speed, his glove, his arm, and his rare poise for someone so young.

"I told [Indians general manager] Hank Greenberg to 'put that kid in right field and forget about it,'" said Rosen, who would later serve as president of the Yankees, Astros, and Giants and is credited with putting together the Giants' 1989 National League pennant winner. "Maris was a terrific young player, not only as a hitter, but he was an outstanding outfielder. He also was, in the parlance of the clubhouse, a 'rock head.' Very stubborn, very headstrong."

Maris knew the Indians were getting old and that they were looking to develop some young talent. He saw that there was an opportunity for a young player to move into the starting lineup immediately, and he believed that by his performance in spring training games, he had earned the right to open the season with the Indians—if not in the starting lineup, at least on the Opening Day roster.

The Indians had other ideas. They believed that in Maris they had a potential star of the future, but they felt that at the age of 21, and with only 25 games above Class A under his belt, he needed more seasoning. They would send him to Indianapolis, their top farm team in the Class AAA American Association.

Not surprisingly, Maris didn't agree. Not only didn't he agree, he decided to do something about it.

"He packed his car and was ready to quit and go home," Rosen remembered. "I got in his car and sat and talked with him for an hour. I told him not to do anything rash, that he should go to Indianapolis, continue doing what he was doing in spring training and that his time would come."

Maris listened and eventually cooled off and reconsidered. He would go to Indianapolis.

Also in the American Association at the time, playing at Charleston, was a tall, slim, 24-year-old right-handed pitcher of great promise from Kentucky by the name of Jim Bunning. He would go on to have a magnificent 17-year major league career with the Detroit Tigers, Philadelphia Phillies, Pittsburgh Pirates, and Los Angeles Dodgers, during which he would win 224 games, pitch 151 complete games, 40 shutouts, and two no-hitters, including a perfect game against the New York Mets in 1964, on Father's Day, fitting because at the time Bunning was the father of seven.

Bunning is one of only five pitchers to throw a no-hitter in each league and the second (the first was the legendary Cy Young) to win 100 games and strike out 1,000 batters in each league. When he retired, Bunning's 2,855 strikeouts were second on the all-time list to another legend, Walter

Johnson. Bunning, who was elected to the Baseball Hall of Fame in 1996, served 12 years in the United States Congress and is a two-term United States Senator from Kentucky.

Bunning remembers Maris as a young minor leaguer who impressed him not only with his power but also with his all-around ability.

"I had trouble with him in Indianapolis, and later I had trouble with him in the major leagues," Bunning recalled. "Rocky Colavito came along at about the same time, but I never had the same trouble with Colavito like I had with Maris. Maybe it was because of the position of my release." Bunning threw three-quarter overhand and occasionally side-armed and was tougher on a right-handed hitter like Colavito than on a lefty batter like Maris.

"As much as I thought of Maris in the minor leagues, I never thought he would ever hit 30 home runs because he wasn't muscular and big like Mickey Mantle," Bunning added. "Roger had kind of a compact build. And his stroke! He didn't swing hard. Later, he developed a swing for Yankee Stadium and that made him the unbelievable threat he was when he was with the Yankees, but he didn't have that kind of swing when I saw him in Indianapolis."

Indeed, at Indianapolis, Maris hit only 17 home runs in 131 games, but he drove in 75 runs and batted .293. His apprenticeship, it appeared, was over.

The Indians' youth movement began in earnest when Colavito, the 22-year-old Bronx-born right-handed power hitter took over as the team's regular right fielder. He had hit 150 home runs in parts of six minor league seasons, had appeared in five games for the Indians the previous year after hitting 30 long ones for Indianapolis, and reached the big leagues to stay in 1956 after playing in 35 games for San Diego in the Pacific Coast League. His powerful throwing arm made him a natural for right field, and he would become one of the premier players at his position, playing 14 major league seasons and recording 123 outfield assists.

In 101 games, Colavito batted .276, belted 21 homers, drove in 65 runs, and finished second to Chicago White Sox shortstop Luis Aparicio in the American League Rookie of the Year voting.

The Indians were convinced they had a bona fide home run slugger and a future star in their rookie right fielder. What's more, they believed they had the perfect left-handed hitting outfield complement to Colavito in Roger Maris, 13 months to the day younger than Colavito.

Chapter Three

Indian Summer

Roger Maris made his major league debut with the Cleveland Indians against the Chicago White Sox in Cleveland Stadium on April 16, 1957. He was 22 years, seven months, and six days old at the time. He batted fifth and played left field. Rocky Colavito, 23, was the Indians' right fielder and cleanup hitter. The center fielder was 29-year-old Al Smith.

In front of a crowd of 31,145, Maris came to bat for the first time with one out in the second inning against left-hander Billy Pierce, 30, a nine-year major league veteran who had won 114 big-league games, 20 of them the previous season. Maris struck out. But he would face Pierce four more times, line three singles and fly out to center field.

The game went 11 innings, the White Sox winning 3–2 with former Indian Larry Doby singling in the winning run. Both pitchers, Pierce and the Indians' 24-year-old left-hander Herb Score, went the distance. Pierce, the winner, allowed eight hits and three walks, struck out nine, and faced 44 batters. Score faced 50 batters, allowed seven hits, walked 11, struck out 10, and took the loss. No pitch counts were recorded in those days, but each pitcher had to have thrown close to 200 pitches. The time of the game was 3:29.

After a day off, the Indians journeyed to Detroit for the Tigers' home opener on April 18. Again Maris played left field and batted fifth. Again, the Indians played into the 11th inning. When Maris came to bat in the top of the 11th against 31-year-old journeyman Jack Crimian, the bases were loaded and Cleveland had pushed across a run to take a tenuous lead. In his first five plate appearances, Maris had struck out against six-year-veteran left-hander Billy Hoeft, lined to first and struck out against future Hall of Famer Jim Bunning, and struck out and walked against Paul Foytack. This time, against Crimian, he connected and drove a pitch into the right-field stands for a grand slam, the first of his 275 major league home runs.

A teammate of Maris' with the 1957 Indians was Joe Altobelli, who would play in 166 major league games with the Indians and Minnesota Twins. Later, he would manage the San Francisco Giants, Baltimore Orioles, and Chicago Cubs, leading the Orioles to their 1983 five-game World Series triumph over the Philadelphia Phillies.

Altobelli also had played alongside Maris with the Indianapolis Indians of the Class AAA American Association in 1955, a team that would produce 24 major leaguers, including Hank Aguirre, Bud Daley, Russ Nixon, and Dave Pope.

At Indianapolis that season, Altobelli out-homered Maris 19–17. But Maris would hit 275 major league home runs. Altobelli hit 5.

"In Indianapolis, you could see that he had the ability to play in the big leagues," Altobelli recalled. "Everybody who saw him liked him. He was no secret, at least not to those of us in the Cleveland organization. It was obvious that the Indians were grooming him to be their center fielder, and when he got to Cleveland, they kind of just handed him the job. One of the reasons they traded Larry Doby was to make room for Roger."

It wasn't that Maris didn't deserve such treatment, Altobelli quickly explained.

"Roger was a very good all-around player, even as a young guy," he said. "He was a hard-nosed player. He could break up a double play in those days. He had a good, accurate arm. He threw runners out, and he ran the bases well. He had pretty good speed for a big guy. He came to play every day. If anything, he tried too hard sometimes and he couldn't match his enthusiasm with his lack of experience. Once he put the pieces all together, he got into the swing of things."

And then there was the "other" Roger Maris, the guy out of uniform.

"He was quiet, not a big talker at all," Altobelli remembered. "He didn't say much. He never pushed himself. He made some friends, but not many. I don't mean he was disliked, but his personality made him pretty much a loner. I was his teammate for about two-and-a-half to three years and I liked him, but we weren't close. We got along, I think, because I was kind of the same as he was. As a player, I didn't say much either. I just tried to go out and play hard, and that's the way Roger was. I really admired him for that, but he was tough to get to know, no question about it.

"He was very serious. He didn't smile a heck of a lot. Remember, he was from Fargo, North Dakota, and they get only about a month of summer, so what was there to smile about?"

Maris started every one of the Indians' first 19 games, against right-handed and left-handed pitchers, usually in left field, occasionally in right field when Colavito would be rested against certain right-handed pitchers.

On May 5, the Indians hosted the Boston Red Sox in a doubleheader. Right-hander Willard Nixon started for the Sox, and Maris was in right field in place of Colavito. The Red Sox won 5–1, which dropped the Indians' record to 8–7, causing manager Kerby Farrell to implement a mild shakeup in his lineup for the second game against right-hander Dave Sisler. To get more punch in the lineup, Al Smith was shifted from center field to third base, Maris played center field for the first time, veteran Gene Woodling played left field, and Colavito returned to right field.

Five days later, the Kansas City Athletics were in Cleveland, and Maris started his fourth straight game in center field. He hit a two-run home run in the second inning. In the third, he reached on an error and was safe at second on another error. When it was his turn to bat in the fifth, Maris was replaced by pinch-hitter Jim Busby. Maris had apparently suffered a pulled hamstring either sliding into second base in the third inning or running down a fly ball in center field. At the time, Maris was hitting a robust .315 with five home runs and 17 RBIs, a pace that might have generated a 40-home run, 100-RBI rookie season had he stayed healthy. He didn't.

He missed 11 games, came back on May 25 to go hitless in four trips against the White Sox, and then missed two more games. When he was ready to resume regular duty it was as a left fielder, but on June 13, the Indians made a trade that would leave Maris as their full-time center fielder. In need of more batting punch from their outfield, the Indians made a one-for-one trade of outfielders with the Baltimore Orioles, sending center fielder Jim Busby, a brilliant defender but a weak hitter, to the Orioles for 28-year-old Dick Williams, a veteran of five major league seasons.

Williams would play 67 games with the Indians before being traded back to Baltimore after the 1957 season. Later, he would play for the Kansas City Athletics, the Orioles again, and the Boston Red Sox in a 13-year career. But it was as a manager for 21 seasons with Boston, Oakland, California, Montreal, San Diego, and Seattle that Williams gained his greatest acclaim, winning 1,571 games, four pennants, and two World Series. Williams was elected to the Hall of Fame as a manager by the Veterans Committee in 2008.

Several other nagging injuries caused Maris to miss 27 more games, and his production declined dramatically. Maris' batting average plummeted and his power diminished. He finished the season with a .235 average, 14 home runs, and 51 RBIs, disappointing numbers after his spectacular start. Maris further alienated himself with Indians general manager Frank Lane when he declined an offer to play winter ball in the Dominican Republic because he believed the proposed salary of $1,000 per month was not enough to justify leaving his young and growing family.

Despite the poor second half of his rookie season—which could be attributed to the rash of injuries—and because he was only 22 years old, Maris was a desirable commodity on the radar of most major league teams. Among those who recognized Maris' potential was no less an authority than Yankees manager Casey Stengel, who salivated over Maris' short, compact swing, one ideally suited for Yankee Stadium's short right-field porch.

After watching the young slugger hit a home run against his Yankees, Stengel mused rhetorically to reporters, "What about the kid in center field? You don't think he has power? He hits a ball pretty good for a young man, and why wouldn't you like to have him if you could?"

So intrigued were the Yankees by Maris' powerful bat, throwing arm, speed, and defensive skills, they assigned their top talent evaluator, Tom Greenwade, to follow the young outfielder and report on his progress. Greenwade had attained legendary status as a scout by the simple expedient of discovering in Spavinaw, Oklahoma, a free agent teenage Adonis named Mickey Mantle and signing him for the Yankees.

*

Lane never did forgive Maris for refusing to play in the Dominican Republic, and when Maris got off to a slow start in 1958, the Indians' general manager decided to trade him—not that Lane ever needed an excuse to make a trade. Known in baseball circles as "Trader Lane" and "The Wheeler Dealer," Lane never met a trade he didn't like. He seemed to espouse the "grass is greener" theory where baseball players were concerned; i.e., he had a higher regard for another team's players than he did for his own.

Rookie Roger Maris, No. 32 of the Cleveland Indians, waits his turn to hit in the batting cage before a game against the Yankees in Yankee Stadium in 1957. Four years later, he would be the talk of baseball when he hit 61 home runs wearing Yankees' uniform No. 9.

(PHOTO BY: KIDWILER COLLECTION/DIAMOND IMAGES/GETTY IMAGES)

In 18 years as a general manager with the Chicago White Sox, St. Louis Cardinals, Cleveland Indians, Kansas City Athletics, and Milwaukee Brewers, Lane would make more than 400 trades, 241 of them in his eight years running the White Sox. Lane also was the catalyst in the 1960 trade of the reigning American League home run champion, Rocky Colavito, from the Indians to the Tigers for the reigning American League batting champion, Harvey Kuenn, for which the fans of Cleveland never forgave him; and of the trade of managers, sending Indians manager Joe Gordon to Detroit in exchange for Tigers manager Jimmy Dykes.

On June 15, 1958, with Maris batting a mere .225 with nine home runs and 27 RBIs in 51 games, Lane traded him to the Kansas City Athletics as the key figure in a deal that also sent journeyman pitcher Dick Tomanek and first baseman Preston Ward to Kansas City for infielder Woodie Held and first baseman Vic Power. Lane agreed to the trade with the proviso that the Athletics not turn around and immediately send Maris to the Yankees, a maneuver Lane believed was inevitable.

Lane had a passionate dislike for the Yankees and their general manager, George Weiss, a curious emotion because Lane's big break in baseball came in 1946 when he was named general manager of the Yankees' top farm team, coincidentally in Kansas City. When he reached the major leagues as general manager with the White Sox and Indians, Lane seemed to resent the Yankees' ability to stockpile players because of their seemingly bottomless financial reservoir.

A year after the trade, Tomanek and Ward were out of baseball, while Held and Power enjoyed lengthy and productive careers. Power, a dark-skinned native of Puerto Rico, had been signed originally by the Yankees. Power performed well in the Yankees' farm system, but when they failed to promote him to the major leagues, the Yankees were accused in some quarters of being racist. After the 1953 season, the Yankees included Power as part of an 11-player trade with the Philadelphia Athletics. At the time, the Yankees had no players of color on their big-league roster. It would be two more years, eight years after Jackie Robinson was called up to the Brooklyn Dodgers, before the Yankees chose a mild-mannered, universally liked, and respected African American from St. Louis named Elston Howard to break the team's color line.

Meanwhile, Power had a long and distinguished career. He was considered a magician with the glove around first base. If he wasn't the best defensive first baseman in the American League in the 1960s, he certainly was the most flamboyant. There are those who saw them play who still regard Power and Gil Hodges as the best right-handed throwing defensive first basemen in baseball history.

Although he balked at leaving Cleveland at first, Maris came to enjoy playing in Kansas City with its friendly, low-key atmosphere, which fit Maris' personality perfectly. In 99 games with the Athletics, he batted .247, hit 19 home runs, and drove in 53, finishing the season with impressive combined numbers of a .240 average, 28 homers, and 80 RBIs.

Content in Kansas City, Maris got off to a blistering start in 1959. On May 17, he was batting .351. In late July, despite suffering an appendicitis attack that would sideline him for almost a month, Maris' average fluctuated between .339 and .345 and he was a serious challenger for the American League batting championship. Weakened by the appendicitis, Maris' average plummeted and his power diminished. He managed to finish with a .273 average, but because he missed 32 games, his RBIs fell off to 72 and his home runs to 16.

"Roger was a terrific young player," Dick Williams recalled. "He could run. He had a great arm, strong and accurate. He was a hell of a defensive player. And he could hit, for average and with power. Roger and I both hit 16 home runs in '59. [Bob] Cerv was our big power hitter. He hit 20. Roger goes to the Yankees and hits 39 home runs in 1960, and I hit 12. The following year, he hit 61 and I hit 8. He was a very underrated player up to that time. He mostly went unknown until the Yankees got hold of him. And the park he was in [Yankee Stadium], that park was built for him because he was nothing but pull, pull, pull."

Aside from his natural talent, what Williams remembered about a young Roger Maris off the field was, "He was a very shy man, just one of the guys, but very quiet."

In 1959, the best of Roger Maris was still ahead of him. Despite his disappointing season, injury- and illness-ridden though it was, he was only 24 years old, and to most baseball people, especially the Yankees, he seemed on the verge of becoming a star.

Chapter Four

Broadway Bound

As much as he hated the thought, Frank Lane—and all of baseball—figured it was inevitable that Roger Maris would end up a Yankee. The signs for such a result were all in place:

- The Yankees wanted Maris, and the Yankees always got what they wanted.
- The Athletics needed money, and the Yankees had money to burn.
- Maris was the property of the Kansas City Athletics, which was tantamount to auditioning a show in Bridgeport before taking it to Broadway.

Lane's worst fear—that the Athletics would send Maris to the Yankees, the team he loathed—was realized on December 11, 1959, when the Yankees and Athletics announced a seven-player trade. It was the sixth deal of the year between the two teams and the 18th since 1955. From the Yankees, the Athletics would receive:

Hank Bauer—a three-time All-Star who had helped the Yankees win nine American League pennants and seven World

Series. Now 37 years old, he would finish his playing career with the Athletics and then be named their manager on June 19, 1961. He would go on to manage the Baltimore Orioles for five years, winning the World Series in 1966, and the Oakland Athletics for one.

Don Larsen—at the age of 30, he was three years past the highlight of his career, the greatest single pitching performance in major league history, a perfect game in the 1956 World Series (the only no-hitter in World Series history). Larsen would post a record of 1–10 for Kansas City in 1960 and win only 25 more games over the next seven seasons for the Athletics, White Sox, Giants, Astros, Orioles, and Cubs.

Marv Throneberry—a Mickey Mantle wannabe who never fulfilled his potential. He batted .250 for Kansas City with 11 home runs and 41 RBIs in 1960 and was traded to Baltimore. Later, he joined the expansion New York Mets and, sarcastically dubbed "Marvelous Marv," became infamous as the sad sack symbol of that expansion team's ineptness.

Norm Siebern—only 26 years old, he enjoyed four productive if not spectacular seasons with the Athletics and moved on to finish out a fine 12-year major league career with the Orioles, Angels, Giants, and Red Sox, making the All-Star team three times.

In exchange, the Yankees received from the Athletics:

Roger Maris—the key man in the trade and the object of affection for the Yankees, who were convinced he was ready to blossom into a star.

Kent Hadley—a one-time promising left-handed-hitting first baseman who hit 34 home runs for Little Rock in

1958. He would play in 55 games for the Yankees in 1960, bat .203 with four home runs and 11 RBIs and would be released after the season.

Joe DeMaestri—a 31-year-old, nine-year major league veteran infielder who was known more for his glove than his bat. After playing in 905 games in seven seasons as the Athletics' regular shortstop, he would appear in only 79 games for the Yankees in 1960 and '61, batting .229 and .146, and retire after the 1961 season.

"I was glad to be going to the Yankees, even though it meant I would be a backup player [to Tony Kubek]," said DeMaestri. "I was going to a team that had a chance to win the World Series [DeMaestri appeared in four games in the 1960 World Series].

"The Yankees roomed me with Kubek, and I would hang out with Tony and Bobby Richardson on the road while Roger was hanging out with Mickey [Mantle] and [Bob] Cerv.

"Roger and I were friends, but we weren't particularly close. Roger was friendly but not outgoing. Like he couldn't relax and let it out. He'd go out after a game with a bunch of players, but it seemed like he never was at ease. He didn't know how to handle the press. He was always wary and suspicious, like 'What does this guy want from me?' And if a reporter asked him something that maybe wasn't the greatest question, Roger would fire back at him. Sometimes he'd say something that just made you cringe. That wasn't a big deal in Kansas City, where there were maybe two or three writers covering the team. But in New York there were dozens from all kinds of papers, a lot of them young and inexperienced writers. And when that 1961 season hit him, Roger had no idea how to deal with it.

"I actually got to spend more time with Roger after we retired than when we were teammates. My family had a Budweiser beer distributorship in northern California and when he retired, Roger had a Budweiser distributorship in Florida, and we would get to see each other at company meetings and conventions. He was out of baseball by then. The pressure was off. He could relax and he was a different guy. I enjoyed spending time with him."

DeMaestri could have returned to the Yankees in 1962 but chose to retire instead. "I thought it was time to get into the family business," he said. "Wouldn't you know that was the year the Yankees played in the World Series in San Francisco, practically in my backyard?"

The owner of the Kansas City Athletics at the time of the big trade was Arnold Johnson, who was often accused of maintaining an incestuous relationship with the Yankees and of being "a Yankee puppet."

A Chicago-born industrialist and eminently successful businessman, Johnson had entered baseball in December 1953 by way of a real estate transaction. He had purchased Yankee Stadium in the Bronx and Blues Stadium in Kansas City, home of the Yankees' top farm team, the Kansas City Blues, which had been a Yankees affiliate since 1937.

In 1954, Johnson bought the financially strapped Philadelphia Athletics and moved the team to Kansas City, ending—at least overtly—his affiliation with the Yankees. Covertly, Johnson was beholden to the Yankees, whose co-owners Dan Topping and Del Webb held a second mortgage totaling $2.9 million on Johnson's properties. In addition, the Del Webb Construction Company won the contract to remodel Johnson's Kansas City Stadium in order for it to meet major league specifications.

Was it any surprise, then, that players shuffled back and forth between New York and Kansas City, with the Yankees, almost without exception, getting the better end of the many trades between the two teams? Of the 37 players who appeared in at least one game with the Yankees in the 1959 season, nine of them—Hector Lopez, Clete Boyer, Enos Slaughter, Jim Pisoni, Art Ditmar, Duke Maas, Ralph Terry, Bobby Shantz, and Ryne Duren—had been obtained by trade or purchase from Kansas City.

The relationship between Athletics owner Arnold Johnson and Yankees co-owners Dan Topping and Del Webb was clearly a conflict of interest, one that should have resulted in suspensions, fines, or, in the least, reprimand. But commissioner Ford Frick did nothing.

*

Most major league players would be ecstatic over being traded to the Yankees, easily the most prestigious and most famous name in all of team sports, a chance to supplement their incomes by joining a team that had won 10 American League pennants and eight World Series in the previous 13 years. Most players would jump at the chance to play in New York, the media, financial, and industrial capital of the world.

Roger Maris was not like most players. A small-town guy in a small-town environment, he despised the hustle and bustle, the noise and the congestion, the bright lights, and dangerous temptations and distractions of the big city. He was content in Kansas City. He had hoped to play the remainder of his career there. He liked the people, the lifestyle, and the relative solitude. He had a rather large and comfortable house for his growing family in Raytown, Mo., a suburb of Kansas City. He cherished the stability of being home for half the baseball season. He was torn between spending so much time away from his family and moving them halfway across the country for six months every year. Ultimately, he opted for leaving his family in Raytown.

To help ease Maris' trepidation about playing and living in the Big City, and to indoctrinate him in all things New York, Julie Isaacson entered the picture and took Maris under his wing. It was a voluntary and selfless gesture done as a favor to an old friend.

Isaacson—a large, bumbling, boisterous, and gregarious man—was president of the Novelty and Toy Workers Union. Although he was not a fierce baseball fan or a baseball groupie, he had somehow befriended Irv Noren when Noren played with the Yankees in the early 1950s. Through Noren, Isaacson met Bob Cerv, and when Maris was traded to the Yankees, it was Cerv who called Isaacson and asked him to "Look after the kid; show him around," and Isaacson, with a heart as big as his body, was only too happy to oblige.

Maris and Isaacson were the oddest of odd couples, an unlikely pairing of men who seemed to come from different worlds. Maris was "L'il Abner," the strong, silent type, a country kid, introverted, private, withdrawn, and suspicious. Isaacson was "Big Julie," a Runyonesque character right off the pages of *Guys and Dolls*. From his accent to his nickname, he was all New York.

Their first meeting must have been a culture shock for each, just like when Joe Buck first encountered Ratso Rizzo in *Midnight Cowboy* or when Felix Ungar hooked up with Oscar Madison in *The Odd Couple*.

"He was wearing a polo shirt, some kind of corduroy jeans, and white Pat Boone shoes," Isaacson remembered. "I said, 'Listen, kid. Yankee ballplayers don't dress like you. I don't think the Yankees are going to like this.'

"Roger said, 'The hell with them. If they don't like the way I look, they can send me back to Kansas City.' That's just the way he was. You couldn't tell Roger what to say or what to wear."

There was nothing similar about them, no common denominator except the coincidental circumstances of their mutual friendship with Irv Noren and Bob Cerv. Except for that, they would never have been brought together, sought each other out or found any reason to bond, and yet Maris and Isaacson would become the closest of friends.

*

In 1959, the Yankees were in an unexpected, unlikely, and unprecedented decline. Starting with the arrival of Casey Stengel as manager in 1949, the Yankees had won five consecutive World Series and nine pennants and seven World Series in 10 years, averaging 97.3 wins a season over that span.

The word around baseball was that Stengel, the "Ol' Perfessor," who would reach his 69th birthday on July 30, had lost his touch. There were reports that during games the old man would frequently doze off on the bench. For the first time in nine years, the Yankees would finish below second place in the eight-team American League, ending up in third place, 15 games behind the Chicago White Sox and 10 games behind the Cleveland Indians with a record of 79–75, their lowest win total in 34 years and the first time in 13 years they had failed to win 90 games.

It wasn't difficult to figure out what the problem was. In 1958, the Yankees had led the American League in batting average at .268, runs scored with 759, and home runs with 164. The following year, they fell to third in batting, fourth in runs, and fourth in home runs. Their three primary outfielders—Norm Siebern, Mickey Mantle, and Hank Bauer—who had produced 68 home runs and 202 RBIs in 1958, would drop off to a combined 51 homers and 167 RBIs. The main culprit was Bauer, who at age 36 batted a feeble .238 with nine home runs and 39 RBIs. Replacing Bauer with a young power hitter was the Yankees' top priority in the off-season, and the player they targeted was Roger Maris.

To fix what was broken, the Yankees made only three transactions during the off-season. They signed 32-year-old infielder Granny Hamner, a 16-year major league veteran, as a free agent and made two deals on December 11, 1959. They signed as a free agent another veteran, 38-year-old Elmer Valo, a left-handed-hitting outfielder who had played 18 seasons with the Athletics, Dodgers, Phillies, and Indians, and they completed the seven-player trade with Kansas City that brought Roger Maris, reluctantly and unhappily, to New York.

Arriving in St. Petersburg, Florida, for spring training, Maris was assigned uniform No. 9, which had been worn by Hank Bauer; Bobby Brown, who later would become American League president; and by Charlie (King Kong) Keller. In Cleveland, Maris had been given uniform No. 32 in 1957. The next year, he was assigned No. 5, a low, single digit number, the kind more befitting a star. In Kansas City, he first was given number 35 but later was assigned No. 3, coincidentally the number worn in New York by Babe Ruth and by that time permanently retired by the Yankees. So he became No. 9 in New York, the number chosen for him by longtime clubhouse manager Pete Sheehy, a wise old man who had been working for the Yankees since the days of Ruth. By awarding Maris such a low number, Sheehy was projecting that the new guy was going to be a star. In such matters, Sheehy was rarely mistaken.

In St. Pete, Maris won no friends among the Yankees or their fans and scored no points for tact when he told the press, "I'm not happy at all coming to New York. I liked Kansas City. I expected to play out my career there."

Maris was further upset when, against his wishes, Stengel assigned him to play left field.

"I just want to see if he can do it," Stengel explained to an inquisitive media, meaning that whereas in most ballparks, right field was where managers wanted their outfielder with the strongest throwing arm, Yankee Stadium's spacious left field required a player not only with a strong arm but one with speed.

If Stengel was acknowledging his exceptional defensive skills by playing him in left field, the compliment was missed by Maris.

"I'm more comfortable in right," he complained. "That's where I played most of my career."

Maris had no illusions that he would displace Mickey Mantle as the Yankees' center fielder, but he had every reason to believe he would take over Bauer's right-field spot. By his remarks about Stengel using him in left field, the members of the press covering the Yankees were learning that they were not going to get platitudes and political correctness from Maris. He was going to speak his mind and let the chips fall where they may.

Ordinarily, a team's won-lost record in spring training games is irrelevant. Not so with the Yankees in the spring of 1960. After their disappointing record the previous year, there was pressure on Stengel to win in Florida and, consequently, a greater focus on the Yankees' exhibition season. As a result, there was a sense of panic when the Yankees finished spring training with a record of 11–21 and headed for Boston to open the season against the Red Sox in Fenway Park on Tuesday afternoon, April 19.

For his part, Maris had hit well in the spring, batting .315, but the anticipated and desired power from his short, compact swing was disturbingly missing as he hit only one home run. Perhaps it was for this reason that when he looked at Stengel's Opening Day lineup, Maris saw that he was penciled in as the Yankees' leadoff hitter. On the other hand, Stengel had long since established his preference for batting a hitter with home run potential (Bauer, Gene Woodling, Joe Collins, Tony Kubek) in the leadoff position on the theory that a quick strike gave a team not only an early lead but a huge psychological boost as well.

Stengel also rationalized his choice of a slugger at the top of the lineup with the logic that batting first could give a hitter an additional 30 to 40 at-bats over the course of a season.

Maris was further mystified by the lineup, because after playing him in left field all through spring training, Stengel had decided to start Maris in right field, his preferred position. Mantle was in center, batting fifth, and Hector Lopez, who had come to the Yankees from Kansas City in a trade on May 26, 1959, was in left field and batted fourth.

In his first at-bat as a Yankee, Maris just missed fulfilling Stengel's design of leading off the game with a home run and settled for a double. In the third inning, he bounced back to the pitcher. He then hit a two-run home run in the fifth, singled home a run in the sixth, belted a solo home run in the eighth, and walked in the ninth, completing a 4-for-5 day in his Yankees debut with two home runs and four RBIs in the Yankees' 8–4 victory.

Maris' home run in the top of the eighth put the Yankees ahead 8–2. In the bottom of the eighth, Ted Williams, 41 years old and playing the second game of his final season, blasted a home run, the 494th of his career and his second of the season. The day before in Washington, D.C., when the Red Sox officially opened the American League season against the Senators, Williams had smashed a solo home run against Camilo Pascual in the first at-bat of that year.

The redoubtable "Teddy Ballgame" would end his final season exactly as he started it, hitting a home run off Jack Fisher of the Baltimore Orioles in the final at-bat of his career on September 28 in Fenway Park. It was Williams' 29th home run of the season and the 521st of his illustrious career. For Fisher it was a distinction, albeit dubious, to have served up the final home run of the great Williams' legendary career. It wouldn't be the last time that Fisher would yield a memorable and historic home run.

Ted Williams, the last batter to hit .400 in a season, poses with Roger Maris, who broke Babe Ruth's single-season record of 60 home runs, before a game at Fenway Park during Williams' final season in 1960. Coincidentally, both hitters wore uniform No. 9. (AP IMAGES)

CHAPTER FIVE

MVP

CASEY STENGEL'S NOBLE Roger Maris–as–leadoff-hitter experiment lasted all of two games. In the second game of the season—and of the experiment—played against the Red Sox in Boston's Fenway Park, Maris had an RBI single that produced the Yankees' only run in a 7–1 defeat. For Game 3 against the Red Sox, Maris was in right field, batting fourth behind Mickey Mantle. He singled twice and scored a run in a 4–0 victory.

After hitting two home runs in his Yankees debut on Opening Day, Maris would go homerless for five games, sit out three other games, and then hit his third home run on April 30 in the Yankees' 10th game of the season, a 16–0 rout of the Orioles in Baltimore. Three days later, he hit home run No. 4 against the Tigers and then went homerless for 12 games.

On May 19, with the Yankees in third place and still in need of longball power, general manager George Weiss returned to his old standby panacea, the Kansas City Athletics, and obtained right-handed slugger Bob Cerv in a one-for-one trade for third baseman Andy Carey. The addition of Cerv, who had hit 38 home runs for Kansas City in 1958, was reportedly to add some much-needed right-handed punch to the Yankees' attack, but there might have been another, more subtle reason for the trade, namely the care, feeding, and well-being of the team's newest star. Not surprisingly, the acquisition of his old Kansas City buddy seemed to energize Maris, who snapped out of his homerless drought with a two-homer game in Chicago on May 21.

Like most home run hitters, Maris was streaky. As soon as he found the range, his home runs would come in bunches. In a 30-game stretch from May 21 to June 18, he hit 15 home runs. Starting with a 5–2 victory over the White Sox on June 7, the Yankees ran off 13 wins in 14 games and jumped out to a game and a half lead over the Orioles.

On June 30, Maris hit his 25th home run, and one sportswriter pointed out that when Babe Ruth set the record for home runs in a season with 60 in 1927, he also hit his 25th on June 30. Further investigation showed that although Ruth hit his 25th home run in the Yankees' 70th game, Maris' 25th came in the Yankees' 66th game, putting him four games ahead of Ruth's record pace. It was the first time Maris' name would be linked with Ruth's…but it would not be the last.

Three weeks later, on July 20, Maris hit his 31st home run in the Yankees' 83rd game, and researchers pointed out that it put him 11 games up on Ruth's record, the Babe having hit his 31st in 1927 on July 24, in the Yankees' 94th game. What all this research failed to take into account was that in 1927, Ruth finished with a flurry, belting 17 homers in the month of September, a torrid home run pace that had left several pursuers thwarted in their bid for the record.

When asked about his chances of beating Ruth's record, Maris replied, "No one is going to beat the Babe's record."

Of more immediate interest than his pursuit of Ruth, on the day Maris hit his 31st home run, Mickey Mantle hit his 23rd, giving Maris an eight–home run lead on his more famous teammate. Although sportswriters and head-line writers had not yet hit upon calling them the "M&M Boys," Mantle and Maris had formed a potent one-two power punch that propelled the Yankees.

On July 22, the White Sox arrived at Yankee Stadium for a showdown, four-game weekend series with first place at stake. The Yankees began the series with a one-game lead on the Sox, but that lead quickly vanished as Chicago pounded out an 11–5 rout on Friday night, won 5–3 on Saturday, and took the first game of the Sunday double-header to open a two-game lead. With a crowd of 60,002 hoping for the best but fearing the worst, a defeat in the second game of the doubleheader would have completed a four-game sweep for the White Sox, opened a three-game lead, and might have buried the Yankees for good.

Pitching the second game of the doubleheader for the White Sox was Herb Score, who only a few years before, with the Cleveland Indians, was considered the most dominant pitcher in the American League and often favorably com-pared with Sandy Koufax of the National League. In his first two major league seasons, Score had won 36 games, pitched seven shutouts, and struck out 508 batters. But on May 7, 1957, Score was hit in the face by a line drive off the bat of the Yankees' Gil McDougald and was never the same thereafter.

Score won only 11 games over the next two years, and on April 18, 1960, he was traded by the Indians to the White Sox for pitcher Barry Latman.

With a run in the second inning and another in the fourth in the second game of the July 22 doubleheader, the White Sox had handed Score a 2–0 lead going into the bottom of the fourth. But that's when the Yankees erupted for three runs with Maris singling home the third run of the inning. In the fifth, Mantle blasted his 24th home run into the right-field upper deck. In the sixth Maris and Mantle both hit RBI singles and Elston Howard drove in a third run with a sacrifice fly to build the Yankees' lead to 7–2 on their way to an 8–2 victory that may have saved their season.

Considering how much he looked forward to getting home to spend time with his young family, even for a little while, it was not surprising that Maris would hit three home runs in two games in Kansas City on August 5–6, his 33rd, 34th, and 35th. He now had 35 home runs in 98 games, putting him eight games ahead of Ruth's record pace.

Although the Yankees surged in the final weeks of the season, Maris became the latest to fall victim to Ruth's torrid September pace of 1927 and to a series of minor injuries. He would hit only four more home runs for the remainder of the season, all of them in September.

No longer a threat to Ruth's record, Maris nonetheless hit a huge home run against Baltimore on September 16. The Orioles had arrived at Yankee Stadium for a four-game series with the two teams in a virtual tie for first place in the American League, the Yankees at 82–57 for a .590 winning percentage, the Orioles at 83–58, a winning percentage of .589. In the fifth inning, with the Yankees ahead 1–0, Maris unloaded a two-run homer off left-hander Steve Barber to pad the lead, and the Yankees went on to a 4–2 victory. The home run was Maris' 39th of the season, and with 14 games remaining, he held a five-homer lead, 39–34, over his teammate Mantle in their race for the American League home run title.

Maris would fail to hit another home run for the remainder of the season while Mantle went on one of his familiar home run binges that would mark his entire career. He hit No. 35 against the Orioles on September 17, his 36th and 37th against Washington on September 20 and 21, and No. 38 against Boston on September 24. The following day the Yankees beat the Red Sox 4–3 and clinched their 25th American League pennant.

The Yankees moved from Boston to Washington for a three-game series against the Senators on September 26–28. Neither Maris nor Mantle was able to leave the park in the first two games, but on September 28, the Yankees faced Washington left-hander Chuck Stobbs, one of Mantle's favorite pitching patsies. Stobbs would serve up eight of Mantle's 536 home runs, tied for the fifth most of any pitcher, including one of the most legendary home runs in baseball history.

It came in Washington in the fifth inning of a game on April 17, 1953. Mantle hit a tremendous drive to left field that sailed clear out of Griffith Stadium. Legend has it that when he saw the majestic blast, Arthur (Red) Patterson, director of public relations for the Yankees, left the press box, went to the street behind the left-field fence, located the spot where the ball had hit, and measured the distance of the home run at an incredible 565'. Because Mantle was becoming famous for prodigious home runs, no one questioned the authenticity of Patterson's discovery (although years later, Mantle confessed that he heard Patterson never left the press box). In any case, it has forever been reported that the home run off Stobbs in 1953 did indeed travel 565' and that it was the shot that introduced into the baseball lexicon the phrase, "tape measure home run."

On September 28, 1960, Mantle hit not one, but two home runs against Stobbs, a two-run shot in the first inning to give the Yankees a 2–0 lead and a solo blast in the fifth. The two home runs surged Mantle past his teammate Maris, 40 home runs to 39. When neither Mantle nor Maris hit a home run in the final three games of the season, Mantle had won his fourth home run title.

∗

Maris' consolation was in the winning of the American League pennant as the Yankees won 49 of their final 69 games, ending the season by winning their last 15 games to finish eight games ahead of the Orioles. Maris had played on a pennant winner for the first time in his career, and he had the satisfaction of knowing he had made a vital contribution toward the winning of that pennant. He also led the American League in RBIs with 112, 18 more than Mantle; extra-base hits; and slugging average and was awarded a Gold Glove for defense. Maris would get his greatest reward that winter when the Baseball Writers' Association of America announced the result of the Most Valuable Player voting.

Twenty-four members of the BBWAA, three from each American League city, served on a panel of MVP voters. They were asked to vote for 10 players, in order of preference, with the vote weighted as follows: 14 points for a first-place vote and then 9, 8, 7...down to 1 point for the 10th player listed. Although Mantle attracted more first-place votes (10) than Maris (8), Maris outpointed Mantle, 225–222, depriving Mantle of winning his third MVP. Baltimore's Brooks Robinson, with three first-place votes and 211 points, finished third.

While the Yankees were breezing to the pennant in the American League, the Pittsburgh Pirates, driven by Roberto Clemente, Dick Groat, and Dick Stuart, were doing likewise in the National League—finishing seven games ahead of the Milwaukee Braves to win their first pennant in 33 years (they had last won in 1927 when they were swept in four games by the Babe Ruth–Lou Gehrig–Bill Dickey– Tony Lazzeri Yankees of Murderers Row).

The World Series of 1960 was one of the most bizarre in history, its tone set in the very first game. In the top of the first inning, in his first World Series at-bat, Maris smashed a home run off 20-game-winner Vern Law to get the Yankees off on the right foot. In that first game, the Yankees hit two home runs to the Pirates' one, rapped out 13 hits to the Pirates' eight, but the Pirates would win the game, 6–4.

As a team, the Yankees batted .338 for the Series, the Pirates .256. The Yankees scored 55 runs to the Pirates' 27, had 91 hits to the Pirates' 60, hit 10 home runs to the Pirates' four, drove in 54 runs to the Pirates' 26. Yankees pitchers had a combined earned run average of 3.54. Pirates pitchers had a combined earned run average of 7.11. The Yankees threw two shutouts, both by Whitey Ford. Pirates pitchers had none.

In the series, Mantle batted .400 with three home runs and 11 RBIs, and Maris batted .267 with two homers and two RBIs. Meanwhile, Dick Groat, who had batted .325 for the Pirates in the regular season, was held to .214 in the Series and Dick Stuart, who hit 23 home runs and drove in 83 runs, was held without a homer or an RBI in the World Series.

And yet the Yankees won three games and the Pirates won four.

So how did the Yankees, who won their three games by the combined margin of 35 runs, lose to the Pirates, who won their four games by the combined margin of seven runs?

The simple answer is that they lost because the Pirates scored more than one-third of their runs in the seventh game because they staged a surprising five-run rally in the bottom of the eighth to wipe out a three-run Yankees lead, and because Bill Mazeroski led off the bottom of the ninth with the first game-winning, World Series–winning home run in history off Ralph Terry.

The not-so-simple answer is that the Yankees lost because Casey Stengel, the legendary managerial genius who had won 10 pennants and seven World Series in 12 years as manager of the Yankees, refused to start his best pitcher, Whitey Ford, in Game 1, which would have enabled him to start three times in the Series.

A sore shoulder had hampered Ford in the early part of the season. By June 21, he had won only two games, but he would come on in the second half of the season, winning nine games after June 21 and finishing strong by winning his last three starts. Nevertheless, Stengel opted to start

The Yankees' venerable manager Casey Stengel walks off Forbes Field in Pittsburgh moments after a home run by the Pirates' Bill Mazeroski ended the seventh game of the 1960 World Series. It would be the last game Stengel ever managed with the Yankees. (Photo by Herb Scharfman/ Sports Imagery/Getty Images)

right-handers Art Ditmar and Bob Turley in the first two games of the World Series in Pittsburgh, electing to save Ford for Game 3 in Yankee Stadium, where left-handers were perceived to have an advantage.

Ford won Game 3 10–0 on a four-hitter and came back four days later in Pittsburgh to beat the Pirates 12–0 on a seven-hitter. The victory forced a seventh game for which Ford was unavailable. When he went to the bullpen late in the game, he was unable to get loose, so he shut it down and was reduced to being a disappointed and disgruntled spectator.

"I was pitching as well as I ever had," Ford said. "I felt I should have started the first game, so that I could pitch three times if it became necessary. Stengel had other ideas. Casey had this thing about saving me for Yankee Stadium to take advantage of the big area in left field and left-center, Death Valley to right-handed hitters. That really ticked me off. It was the only time I ever got mad at Casey."

Losing that World Series, especially the way it was lost, was a bitter disappointment to veteran Yankees.

"We were clearly the much better team," said Mickey Mantle. "The scores of the games point that out. I never felt so bad in my life. I cried all the way home on the plane from Pittsburgh to New York. That was the only time in my professional career that I actually cried after losing."

Chapter Six

Major Changes

Even before they dropped the ball on New York's Times Square on December 31, 1960, numerologists were telling us that the year 1961 was going to be special. It would be the first "upside-up" year since 1881—i.e., a year in which its numerals would read the same if you turned them upside down—and the last such numerical phenomenon until the year 6009.

In addition, the year 1961 was marked by change. On the 20th day of the New Year, a youthful, energetic, and vibrant John Fitzgerald Kennedy was inaugurated as the 35th president of the United States, succeeding Dwight D. Eisenhower. At age 43 years and 236 days, 27 years Eisenhower's junior, Kennedy became the youngest elected United States president, bringing with him into office a new spirit of hope and vitality.

In baseball, there also were changes. The American League was expanding to 10 teams and, for the first time, had a franchise on the West Coast, the expansion Los Angeles Angels, later to become the California Angels and then the Los Angeles Angels of Anaheim. The Washington Senators had relocated to Minneapolis–St. Paul and had become the Minnesota Twins. To fill the void of baseball in the nation's capital, Washington, D.C., was awarded an expansion franchise to be called the Washington Senators just like its recently dear departed.

To accommodate the new 10-team league and maintain an equal number of games between teams, the American League announced its schedule would expand from 154 games to 162. There was no word from the American League, or the Commissioner's office, how the expanded schedule would affect baseball's record keeping, which had been in force for almost a century.

In New York, the Yankees were starting their fourth and final year as the city's only major league team—the New York Mets would begin play the following season when the National League also was to expand to 10 teams. Three years earlier, in 1958, the Brooklyn Dodgers had relocated to Los Angeles and the New York Giants to San Francisco, leaving New York City with fewer than two baseball teams for the first time since 1882, the year before the New York Gothams joined the National League and the New York Metropolitans joined the American Association and shared the city.

*

Now the Yankees, still smarting from their defeat by the Pittsburgh Pirates in the 1960 World Series, were undergoing some sweeping changes of their own. They would be introducing a new manager when they reported to spring training, which they would hold in St. Petersburg, Florida, for the final time. The Yankees announced that in 1962, they would move to a new training facility in Fort Lauderdale, across the state on Florida's east coast, after having spent 14 of the previous 15 springs in St. Petersburg (the exception being 1951 when they trained in Phoenix, Arizona).

On the morning of October 18, 1960, five days after the final game of the 1960 World Series, the Yankees summoned the press to Le Salon Bleu in the posh Savoy Hilton Hotel on Fifth Avenue for "an important announcement." It was generally believed the "important announcement" was going to be nothing monumental, merely that Charles Dillon (Casey) Stengel, age 70 years, two months, and 18 days, the man who had guided the Yankees to 10 American League pennants and seven World Series titles in 12 years, had signed on once again to manage the Yankees in 1961 on a one-year contract (standard for the Yankees at the time) with a substantial raise.

Few, if any, in the gathering crowd were prepared for the bombshell that was dropped after Bob Fishel, the Yankees' Director of Public Relations, called for attention and then introduced the team's co-owner, Dan Topping.

"Casey Stengel has been, and deservedly so, the highest paid manager in baseball history," Topping began. "Casey Stengel has been, and is, a great manager. He is being well rewarded with $160,000 to do with as he pleases."

"Do you mean he's through? Resigned?" came a voice from the crowd.

Suddenly Stengel was on his feet, inching toward the microphone, and shouting, "Now wait a minute for chris-sakes and I'll tell ya.

"I was paid up in full. Mr. [Del] Webb [Yankees' co-owner] and Mr. Topping have started a program for the Yankees. They needed a solution as to when to discharge a man on account of age. My services are no longer required by this club, and I told them if this was their idea, not to worry about me."

"Were you fired?" persisted a voice from the back of the room.

"Resigned, fired, quit, discharged, use whatever you damn please. I don't care. You don't see me crying about it."

Hours later, after most of the reporters had left, Stengel remained behind, talking with old friends.

"I commenced winning pennants when I came here," he said somewhat wistfully, "but I didn't commence getting any younger."

With that, a brilliant chapter in the history of the New York Yankees had come to a close and another was about to begin.

*

Two weeks after Stengel's ouster, on November 3, the Yankees made it a clean sweep by replacing general manager George Weiss with Roy Hamey. Weiss had joined the Yankees in 1932 and by building the farm system, beefing up the scouting corps, and making shrewd trades, he brought the team unparalleled success with 19 pennants and 15 World Series championships in 29 years. Weiss, however, was a notorious penny-pincher when it came to players' salaries (it was reported he was paid bonuses on the basis of the team's bottom line) and was reputed to be a humorless loner with few close friends.

When he mentioned Weiss in his column, Jimmy Cannon always referred to him as "Lonesome George

Weiss, the friendless general manager of the Yankees."

Soon after he was let go by the Yankees and had slipped into retirement, Weiss' wife, Hazel, commented, "I married George for better or for worse but not for lunch."

In Weiss' successor, the Yankees chose his polar opposite. Roy Hamey was well-liked, gregarious, and a genial host who had come up through the Yankees' system in a variety of executive roles in the minor leagues, then returned to the organization to serve as assistant general manager in 1959

Roger Maris signs his 1961 Yankees contract with the approval of the team's general manager, Roy Hamey. In his record-breaking season, Maris earned $37,500. (AP IMAGES)

and 1960. He spent five years as general manager of the Pittsburgh Pirates and five more as GM of the Philadelphia Phillies, but his teams never finished higher than fourth place.

To succeed Stengel, the Yankees chose Ralph George Houk, a 41-year-old, cigar-smoking former catcher who was born and raised on a farm in Stull, Kansas, 10 miles outside of Lawrence, the home of the University of Kansas. He had been in the Yankees' organization as player, coach, and minor league manager for 23 years, minus four years in military service. Houk was an attractive and much sought-after managerial prospect. Inquiries about Houk's availability from other teams may have had as much to do with hastening the decision to force Stengel out as losing the World Series to the Pirates or the growing belief that the baseball parade had passed the old man by.

Houk's playing career had been spectacularly mediocre. He spent parts of eight seasons with the Yankees, one of a veritable graveyard of catchers that grew old, frustrated, and unfulfilled playing behind Yogi Berra (Sherman Lollar, Gus Triandos, Charlie Silvera, Lou Berberet, Gus Niarhos, Ken Silvestri, Clint Courtney, Darrell Johnson, and Jesse Gonder are among those who played behind Berra).

In those eight seasons, Houk appeared in 91 games, an average of fewer than 12 games per season, came to bat 158 times, had 43 hits, no home runs, 20 RBIs, and an average of .272. All those years of sitting and observing from the bench, however, helped Houk hone an acute knowledge of baseball. In addition, he was perceived to be a leader of men based largely on an impressive military record. During World War II, Houk served as a Ranger with the Ninth

Armored Division. He was wounded in the Battle of the Bulge, awarded the Silver Star, and earned several decorations and a battlefield commission to the rank of Major.

When his playing career ended, the Yankees made him manager of their farm team in Denver in the Class AAA American Association. He finished third in his first season, second in his second season, and second again in his third season in which he led the Denver Bears to the American Association playoff championship and the Little World Series, an annual competition at the time that paired the champion of the American Association against the champion of the International League to produce an overall minor league champion.

In 1958, Houk was brought back to New York to serve as Stengel's first-base coach, manager-in-waiting, and the designated replacement for Stengel when the old man was ejected from a game or was unable to manage due to illness. Houk soon earned a reputation as someone not to cross. On the train trip returning from the Yankees' 1958 World Series victory in Milwaukee things got a little rowdy during the victory celebration. Relief pitcher Ryne Duren, having celebrated a little too much and having become somewhat too exuberant, thought it would be fun to smash Houk's omnipresent cigar in his face. Houk didn't appreciate the humor and he decked Duren. From that point on, the word was out that you don't mess with "The Major," a reputation that would serve him in good stead as a manager.

Houk was mindful of the fact that he was stepping into huge shoes in replacing Stengel, who not only won pennants and World Series, he did it while being the consummate charmer, raconteur, and double talker. As one baseball executive put it, "That's an awful load for a guy to haul. To begin with, Ralph's no comedian, and if he does win, the best he gets is a Mexican standoff, a dead heat. He's expected to win; that's what Casey always did."

Despite his reputation for toughness and intimidation, Houk soon also became known as a player's manager. As if eager to prove he was his own man, or to put his personal stamp on his administration, Houk, the rookie manager, would make two significant moves that would prove to have a profound effect not only on the American League pennant race, but on baseball history: he put Whitey Ford, who had pitched on a five-day rotation under Stengel, on a four-day schedule (Ford responded with his best season, a record of 25–4 and the Cy Young award); and he switched Maris' and Mantle's batting positions.

The switch was not intended as an accommodation to Maris, nor was it done to aid Maris. Rather it was made with Mantle as the focal point. Since he became established as the Yankees leader and best player in 1952, Mantle had batted in the No. 3 position. When Maris arrived, Stengel installed the new man in the No. 4 position, behind Mantle. But Houk viewed batting Mantle fourth as an opportunity to capitalize on the switch-hitter's enormous power and talent to get more production from him. Houk consulted with Mantle and suggested the move, reasoning that Mantle would do his customary damage in any spot in the batting order, but that batting fourth would afford him greater opportunity for driving in runs. Mantle, always the team player, readily agreed to the move. He would be willing to subordinate his own comfort for the good of the team.

At first, Mantle batted fourth and Houk tried a variety of players as his No. 3 hitter. In the team's first 29 games in 1961, Maris would bat third 11 times, fifth 7 times, sixth once, and seventh (always against a left-handed pitcher) 10 times, while Hector Lopez batted third 7 times, Yogi Berra 5 times, and Tony Kubek, Clete Boyer, and Bob Cerv each batted third twice. In those 29 games, Mantle batted .307 with 10 home runs and 26 RBIs, and the Yankees were 16–12 with one tie and in second place, five games behind Detroit.

Later, when Maris had become a serious home run threat, Houk moved him into the three hole to stay, theorizing that with Mantle batting behind him, Maris would be certain to get better pitches to hit. Houk proved to be prescient, as Maris, even while he was challenging Babe Ruth's single-season home run record, walked 32 fewer times than Mantle and didn't receive an intentional walk all season.

The team that Houk welcomed in the spring of 1961 was a powerhouse and the clear favorite to win a second consecutive pennant. In addition to Mantle, the defending American League home run champion, and Maris, the 1960 American League RBI king and Most Valuable Player, Houk had Moose Skowron at first base, Bobby Richardson at second, Tony Kubek at shortstop, and Clete Boyer at third base. Elston Howard and John Blanchard would handle the bulk of the catching with Yogi Berra in reserve, while Berra shared left field with Hector Lopez with an occasional start for Bob Cerv, Blanchard, and Jack Reed. The pitching staff, headed by Ford, also included Ralph Terry, Bill Stafford, and Roland Sheldon with Luis Arroyo and Jim Coates in the bullpen.

*

If the Yankees were upbeat about their prospects for the 1961 season as spring training began, there was another reason that caused excitement in the Yankees' training camp, the appearance of movie goddess Marilyn Monroe. The beauteous Marilyn had been married to Yankees icon Joe DiMaggio, who was with the team in spring training listed as a special hitting instructor. In truth, he was there for public relations purposes and because owners Dan Topping and Del Webb were fulfilling a financial commitment to keep the team's greatest living player involved with the Yankees.

DiMaggio had wed Monroe in 1954, but the marriage lasted all of 274 days. However, the divorce was amicable and the two remained friends. Monroe had later married the Pulitzer Prize–winning playwright Arthur Miller (*Death of a Salesman*), but that marriage was falling apart in the spring of 1961. DiMaggio invited Marilyn to St. Petersburg to "get away from it all," to relax, and to help her get through this difficult time in her life.

At the request of Moose Skowron, DiMaggio and Marilyn joined a group of Yankees, including Tony Kubek, Yogi Berra, and Skowron, for dinner on two successive evenings. They were two nights that the players have never forgotten.

*

Although the Yankees of 1961 had everything, power, pitching, and defense—and the thrill of meeting the famous and ravishing Marilyn Monroe—they nonetheless stumbled badly through spring training. In their final game of the spring in Florida—and their final game as a home team in St. Petersburg—the Yankees scored a run in the bottom of the 11th inning on singles by Boyer, Skowron, and Maris to beat the Cardinals 5–4. It left them with a record of 9–17 with three games remaining against the Cardinals in St. Louis—the Yanks would lose the first two, and the third game would be rained out, leaving their spring record at 9–19.

Despite their horrible record, Houk put on his optimistic face in an interview with John Drebinger of the *New York Times* and predicted another American League pennant.

"As of now I see no reason to think otherwise," Houk told Drebinger. "I know our won-lost record has been anything but spectacular. But I've never been concerned about that. Our primary purpose this spring was to get in shape for the pennant race. With this in mind, I'm completely satisfied. Furthermore, I'm prepared to go with what we have. We don't expect any trades."

Houk said he was pleased with the way Roger Maris finally seemed to have snapped out of a batting slump that plagued him in the early part of spring training.

"He's hitting the ball hard," Houk said. "And with Mickey Mantle, Bill Skowron, Yogi Berra, and others also meeting the ball, we're going to score some runs.

"As for the pitching, with everybody in shape, I'm not worrying about that, either. I'd say we're ready to go."

It was what would come to be known as typical Houk bravado, acquired, no doubt, during his military career— Never show doubt, fear, or concern.

Privately, Houk had other thoughts.

"When we started playing games in the spring and we couldn't win," he said, "I was beginning to wonder what I had gotten myself into."

CHAPTER SEVEN

Slow Start

ON APRIL 11, 1961, RALPH HOUK awoke at 7 AM in his rented century-old farmhouse in the tony suburban town of Saddle River, New Jersey, the town President Richard Nixon later called home after he left office.

After a leisurely breakfast prepared by his wife Bette, Houk left home at 8:30 for the trip into the Bronx. At the George Washington Bridge toll booth, the toll taker recognized the new Yankees manager and wished him luck while taking Houk's 50¢ toll.

Because of early morning commuter traffic, it took Houk 45 minutes to make the 20-mile trip to Yankee Stadium. He pulled into the players' parking lot shortly before 9:30, walked past the handful of early arriving fans to the press gate and into the Stadium and then descended a short flight of stairs on his way to the home team's clubhouse.

Only the clubhouse men, Pete Sheehy and his assistant Pete Previte, plus one or two players were in the clubhouse when Houk entered the manager's office that had been entirely remodeled. Gone were the reminders of the previous

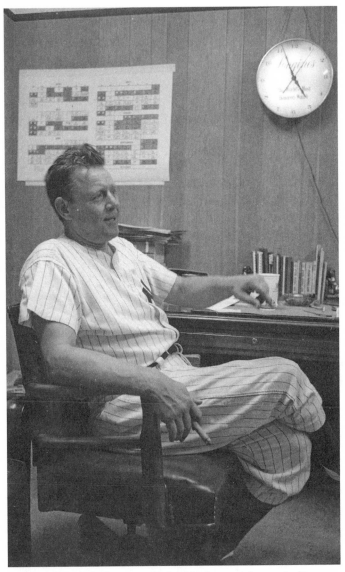

"The Major," Yankees' manager Ralph Houk, meets the press in his Yankee Stadium office after a game. (Photo by C&G Collections/Getty Images)

administration under Casey Stengel—the photos and the old roll-top desk that had been used by every Yankees manager since Miller Huggins. The room had been enlarged and paneled in gray.

"I had nothing to do with it," Houk demurred sheepishly. "I knew nothing about it. This is the way I found the place when we got back from spring training."

On April 11, 1961, the trial of Nazi Adolf Eichmann began in Jerusalem, but that was of little interest to the gathering crowd in Yankee Stadium halfway across the world in the Bronx, New York. There, on an unseasonably raw and windy Tuesday afternoon in Yankee Stadium, Ralph Houk was making his official debut as manager of the Yankees against the Minnesota Twins in their first game as a member of the American League after the organization's move from Washington, D.C.

This was the starting lineup Houk presented for his first game to home-plate umpire Bill McKinley:

Bobby Richardson, 2b
Hector Lopez, lf
Yogi Berra, c
Mickey Mantle, cf
Roger Maris, rf
Bill Skowron, 1b
Tony Kubek, ss
Clete Boyer, 3b
Whitey Ford, p

The frigid weather only partially accounted for several casualties—the absence of some 55,000 fans as an embarrassingly meager crowd of only 14,607 attended the season opener, and New York City Mayor Robert Wagner, who begged off throwing out the season's first ball because of illness (or because he learned there weren't going to be enough voters in attendance to justify the trip) and sent Bronx Borough President James Lyons to handle the assignment in his stead.

Despite the miserable weather and the small crowd, the Yankees went through the traditional formality of Opening Day ceremonies. The Manhattan College Air Force ROTC band, color guard, and drill team led the procession to center field where the American flag was raised and the band accompanied singer Stuart Foster, who offered the national anthem, after which two additional flags were raised—the 1921 American League pennant, the Yankees' first, and the 1960 American League pennant, their 25th.

The procession then moved to home plate. Seated in a box seat adjacent to the Yankees' dugout were the three "First Ladies of Baseball": Mrs. Babe Ruth, Mrs. Lou Gehrig, and Mrs. John J. McGraw, widow of the late owner/manager of the New York Giants. They saw Dick Young of the *New York Daily News,* chairman of the New York Chapter of the Baseball Writers' Association of America, present Roger Maris with the 1960 American League Most Valuable Player trophy and members of the Yankees' 1960 team receive mementoes commemorating their American League pennant. The players and coaches were given their choice of a watch or a ring. Most of them chose the ring.

After Bronx Borough President Lyons threw out the first ball (he hit a photographer), it was time to "Play ball!"

Also missing on this Opening Day was the Yankees' offense, which managed only three hits—singles by Berra, Skowron, and Ford—against the Twins' Cuban-born right-hander, Pedro Ramos.

Ramos and Ford had dueled through six scoreless innings until the Twins broke through against Ford with three runs in the seventh and coasted to a 6–0 victory. It was a shocking development to partisans of the home team, many of whom were aware that it was the first time in seven years that the Yankees lost a home opener; that Ford had a career record of 24–5 against the Washington Senators, now the Minnesota Twins; and that since joining the Yankees, he had been the starting pitcher in five home openers and had won all five, pitching four complete games, allowing just four runs and 25 hits and striking out 30 batters in 43 innings. However, history could not help Ford, or the Yankees, on this day.

Maris was hitless in three at-bats. He reached on left fielder Jim Lemon's error in the first, struck out in the fourth, and flied to right in the seventh.

Mantle was hitless in four trips. The night before at the Yankees' annual "Welcome Home" dinner, Mantle, whose 320 career home runs placed him eighth on baseball's all-time home run list, had received an award named for Tom Greenwade, the scout who discovered Mantle on an Oklahoma sandlot.

"I'm sitting there wondering who they're talking about and who they're gonna give the plaque to," said Mantle. "Then I find out it's me."

"I'da died," said Roger Maris. "If they ever call on me without warning, I won't say a word. Even if I know in advance, they still won't get much."

In his first game of 1961 against Ramos, a pitcher he had punished during his career (24 hits in 66 at-bats, an average of .364, 14 RBIs, eight homers) Mantle grounded to second in the first inning, struck out in the fourth and sixth, flied out to end the game, and was roundly booed by the home crowd. Not a good start to Houk's Mantle-as-cleanup-hitter experiment.

Snow and cold weather would cause the Yankees to wait four days for their next game. On April 15, they beat the Kansas City Athletics 5–3. Maris singled and walked in four trips to the plate, but Mantle was 0–3 and was hitless in his first seven at-bats of the season.

Two days later, on April 17, as the nation was riveted by the Bay of Pigs invasion of Cuba, Mantle's bat came alive, as it often did when his buddy, Ford, was the Yankees' pitcher. He hit a two-run homer in the first, singled twice, and walked, driving in all of the Yankees' runs in a 3–0 victory over Kansas City. Ford went the distance on a three-hitter for his first win of the season, which, because of continuing frigid weather, was witnessed by only 1,947 spectators, the lowest attendance at Yankee Stadium in seven years.

After rain and cold weather forced cancellation of the first two games of a scheduled three-game series against the Los Angeles Angels, the Yankees and Angels made up one of the games in a doubleheader on April 20, the day future Yankees star Don Mattingly was born in Evansville, Indiana. The Yankees swept the doubleheader 7–5 and 4–2 and then ran their winning streak to five with a 4–2 win in their first road game of the year against the Orioles.

The winning streak ended with a 5–3 defeat in Baltimore, which was followed by a rain-shortened 5–5 tie and a 4–1 defeat by another of the Orioles' promising young pitchers, Chuck Estrada.

From there it was on to Detroit where the Yankees were joined by their new general manager, Roy Hamey. If this was a sign of panic, it may have crept into the psyches of Yankees players as they managed only seven hits off nemesis Frank Lary in a 4–3 defeat on April 24. The loss left the Yankees with a pedestrian record of 5–4 with one tie after 10 games and dropped them into fourth place, three games behind the first-place Tigers, who ran off their eighth straight win. It made the Yankees sit up and take notice of the men from Detroit, a team that had finished in sixth place, 26 games out of first, the previous season.

Through the first 10 games of the 1961 season, Maris was struggling. Writing in the *New York World-Telegram and Sun,* Dan Daniel said that Maris "wasn't hitting the size of his breakfast check, which usually comes to $1.70." In fact, Maris had a batting average of .161, on five hits in 31 at-bats, no home runs and just one RBI. Mantle, on the other hand, was off to a flying start. After going hitless in his first seven at-bats of the season, he went on a .440 clip with 11 hits in 25 at-bats. After 10 games, he had hiked his average to .344 and had five home runs and 11 RBIs.

Maris hit his first home run of 1961 on April 26 in the Yankees' 11th game of the season. It came in the fifth inning off right-hander Paul Foytack as the Yankees started a four-game winning streak and a stretch of eight wins in nine games with a 13–11 slugfest over the Tigers in Detroit. Mantle clouted two more homers, his sixth and seventh (No. 6 came left-handed off Jim Donohue and No. 7 came right-handed off Hank Aguirre. It was the eighth time Mantle had hit home runs from each side of the plate in the same game. He would do it two more times, in 1962 and 1964, for a major league record of hitting home runs from each side of the plate in one game 10 times) and drove in four runs to jump-start the Yankees on a four-game winning streak.

The following day, the Yankees returned home and beat the Indians 4–3 as Mantle excelled on both offense and defense. His sacrifice fly in the bottom of the fifth gave the Yankees a 3–2 lead. The Indians tied it in the top of the sixth, but in the bottom of the seventh, the Yankees, and Mantle, capitalized on some questionable strategy by Indians' manager Jimmie Dykes.

There were two outs, Tony Kubek on second, left-hander Johnny Antonelli on the mound, and right-hander Barry Latman warming in the bullpen with Mantle due to bat. Dykes went to the mound, and it appeared his mission was to replace Antonelli with Latman, who would be ordered to walk Mantle intentionally and try to retire the next batter, Moose Skowron, to end the inning. But when Dykes left the mound, he had not taken Antonelli with him. The left-hander was going after Mantle.

Mantle swung at Antonelli's first pitch and drove to the 407' sign in the right-center gap for a triple that scored Kubek with what would prove to be the winning run. But before the Yankees could put the game in the "win" column, it had to be saved, and it was Mantle who saved it.

In the top of the ninth, Willie Kirkland singled with two out. Bubba Phillips followed with a smash to deep right-center that had extra bases written all over it. Pinch runner Mudcat Grant was off with the crack of the bat, and it appeared the ball would split the outfielders and Grant would come around to score the tying run. However, Mantle, using his world-class sprinter's speed, raced after the ball, lunged, slipped, skidded, caught the ball in the webbing of his glove, and held on for the final out of the game.

Three days later in Washington on Sunday, April 30, the Yankees won their fourth straight in the first game of a doubleheader as Ford beat Dick Donovan 4–3 with relief help from Bill Stafford and Luis Arroyo, for his third win in four decisions. Maris had a single in five trips. Mantle also had a single in four at-bats, stole two bases, and scored the Yankees' first run.

The winning streak ended in the second game of the doubleheader when veteran left-hander Hal Woodeshick and two relievers, Dave Sisler and Pete Burnside, beat the Yankees 2–1. Maris had a double in four at-bats, Mantle a single in four at-bats, and the Yankees remained a game behind the Tigers, who split a doubleheader with Baltimore.

$$*$$

The big news of the day in baseball on April 30, 1961, however, was out of Milwaukee. Against the hometown Braves, the Giants' Willie Mays became the ninth player in history to hit four home runs in a game, a magnificent performance witnessed by only 13,114 that caused the melancholy New York Giants fans to reflect on what they were missing and lament what might have been had the Giants not moved to San Francisco.

Mays hit a solo home run off Lew Burdette in the first inning and a two-run homer off Burdette in the third. In the sixth he got Seth Morehead for a three-run shot, and in the eighth, he belted a two-run homer off Don McMahon, an eight-RBI game and a 14–4 victory. Mays just missed what would have been a fifth home run in the fifth inning when he drove a ball to center field that was caught at the fence by Henry Aaron, and he was on deck when Jim Davenport made the Giants' final out in the ninth inning.

Ten home runs were hit in the game, eight by the Giants (four by Mays, two by Jose Pagan, and one each for Orlando Cepeda and Felipe Alou). Aaron hit two home runs for the Braves and drove in all four of his team's runs.

The four–home run explosion boosted Mays' season total to six (Mantle had seven at the time and Maris one), but Mays was not under the same scrutiny as Mantle and Maris because the National League still had eight teams and a 154-game schedule (expansion would come to the National League a year later). Mays would finish his career in 1973 with 660 home runs, third on the all-time list, but his name never entered the discussion when it came to forecasting who might challenge Ruth's single-season record. Mays hit 40 homers in 1961 and four years later reached a career high with 52 home runs.

When the Dodgers and Giants were still in New York, the city's baseball fans were blessed to have three of the game's all-time greatest center fielders playing within the city limits at the same time, Willie Mays in Manhattan with the Giants, Mickey Mantle in the Bronx with the Yankees, and Duke Snider in Brooklyn with the Dodgers. The proximity to each other of these three future Hall of Famers gave rise to endless debates (and to a song, "Willie, Mickey, and The Duke," written and recorded by "Baseball's Balladeer" Terry Cashman) over which of the three was the greatest. The irony of it all was that despite their rivalry, the three men were friends. Mays and Snider even became teammates with the San Francisco Giants in 1964. In retirement, Mantle and Mays occasionally got together to share their mutual passion for playing golf.

Years after they had retired from the game, Mays, Mantle, and Snider were honored by the New York Chapter of the Baseball Writers' Association of America at its annual dinner. Sitting on the dais, each of the three New York superstar center fielders would rise, walk to the podium, and address a crowd of more than 1,200 fans. When it was Mantle's turn, he said, "They used to argue in New York about who was the best center fielder, but to me there was no argument. Willie was the best. Isn't that right, Duke?"

With that, Mantle looked at Snider, who was nodding his head emphatically.

*

Maris waited seven days after hitting his first home run of 1961 to hit his second, a three-run shot in Minnesota to help the Yankees gain a measure of revenge with a 7–3 defeat of their Opening Day conqueror, Ramos. It came on May 3, in the Yankees' 17th game. At the time, Mantle had eight homers. Their victory over the Twins coupled with the Tigers' 5–4 defeat by the Senators in Washington, moved the Yankees into a tie with the Tigers for first place in the American League.

Three days later, after a 5–3 defeat to the Angels in Los Angeles, the first of three straight defeats, the Yankees dropped out of first place and in the next eight weeks would return to first place only briefly, on June 15. Coinciding with the mini-slump was a hitless streak of 18 at-bats for Mantle.

On May 12, the Tigers came to Yankee Stadium and took the first two games of a four-game series 4–3 and 8–3, the first sign that Detroit was going to be a stubborn foe and a legitimate pennant contender all season.

In the series opener, Detroit's Frank Lary went the distance, stranded 14 runners, and improved his record to 5–1 and his career record against the Yankees to 24–8. To embellish a gutty pitching performance, with the Yankees leading 3–2 in the seventh, Lary doubled and scored the tying run. He led off in the top of the ninth with the score tied 3–3 and belted what proved to be the game-winning home run off Jim Coates. It was the sixth, and last, home run of Lary's career and the only one he would hit all season.

No sooner had Lary's blast disappeared into the seats that a rumpus erupted in the stands behind the visiting team's dugout that caught the attention of the Tigers, who popped out of their dugout seats to see what was going on. Noticing that his father was involved in the altercation, Rocky Colavito, the Tigers' Bronx-born left fielder, bolted from the dugout and ran into the stands to come to the aid of his father. As a result, Colavito was ejected from the game.

"What was I supposed to do," wondered Colavito, "let my 60-year-old father get beat up?"

The Yankees rebounded to take the final two games of the four-game series against the Tigers, but then they lost five of their next six games and fell to third place, five-and-a-half games out of first with a record of 17–15.

More disturbing, the Yankees seemed to be finding new ways to lose games.

On May 9 in Kansas City, Whitey Ford and Luis Arroyo blew a three-run lead when the Athletics scored four runs in the bottom of the eighth and turned a 4–1 deficit into a 5–4 victory.

On May 19, the Yankees took a 7–4 lead into the bottom of the eighth inning in Cleveland when the Indians erupted for five runs. In the inning, Moose Skowron and Clete Boyer both dropped foul pop-ups off the bat of catcher John Romano on consecutive pitches. With the bases loaded, Jim Coates hit Woodie Held with a pitch to force in the go-ahead run, and Vic Power followed by stealing home for an insurance run.

On May 21, against the Orioles at Yankee Stadium, Mantle misjudged a fly ball off the bat of Jim Gentile in the seventh inning that fell for a double and started the Os on a two-run rally to give them a 3–2 victory.

Some writers were questioning Houk's ability to manage and the team's decision to dump Stengel. Others suggested that the Yankees should atone for their mistake by firing Houk on the spot and send out an urgent call to Stengel, in retirement and sitting at home in Glendale, California.

On May 16, Maris was hitting .208 with three home runs and 11 RBIs. Writing in *The Sporting News,* Joe King said, "Ralph Houk has to be wondering about Maris. Which Maris would he be, the MVP who showed .320 with 27 homers and 69 RBIs in the first half of 1960, or the ordinary batsman who fell to .239 with 12 homers and 43 RBIs in the second half of that season?"

Most home run hitters are streaky, and Maris was no exception. In mid-May, his bat started smoking, and the home runs came in bunches. From May 17 through May 31, he hit nine home runs in 13 games. On May 19 in Cleveland, in the Yankees' 30th game, Maris moved into the third batting position to stay and blasted a two-run homer in the first and a single in the sixth. He would bat third for the remainder of the season with the exception of three games in which he moved down to hit cleanup in Mantle's absence.

Curiously, it was during this hot streak, on May 22, that Maris went to see an optometrist. Concerned about Roger's slow start, Yankees' owner Dan Topping and general manager Roy Hamey conjectured that Maris' problems at-bat might have something to do with his eyesight. So they scheduled an appointment with an optometrist and instructed Maris to make the appointment.

Maris didn't feel the need to go, but he had no choice. Such was life for the players in the pre–Marvin Miller, pre–Players Association, and pre-agent days. When the owner who paid your salary and the general manager suggested something, you had no choice but to comply.

During his examination, the optometrist administered drops in Maris' eyes, and when Roger reported to Yankee Stadium for that night's game against the Orioles, his eyes were badly irritated. He started in right field, and fortunately no ball was hit to him in the first inning. When the Yankees came to bat in the bottom of the first, Maris complained to Houk that he couldn't see. Houk sent Blanchard up to bat for Maris, who left the game (he would miss only two other games all season). It was later discovered that the eye drops had caused an infection in Maris' eyes.

Said Houk: "We finally get Roger hitting—and I mean hitting better than he has all year—and he shows up blind."

On May 30, Memorial Day in Boston's Fenway Park, the Yankees demolished the Red Sox 12–3 with a seven–home run barrage, two each for Mantle, Maris, and Skowron, and one for Berra. It was only the fifth time in major league history that three teammates each hit two home runs in the same game.

Mantle hit his 12th home run of the season off Gene Conley in the first inning. In the third, Maris connected for his 10th home run off Conley. In the eighth against Mike Fornieles, Maris and Mantle hit back-to-back home runs for the first time that season (they would do it twice more, against Early Wynn in Chicago on July 13, and against Frank Baumann of the White Sox in Yankee Stadium on July 25). With the Yankees safely ahead in the ninth inning, Mantle was replaced in center field by Jack Reed.

*

Jack Burwell Reed, who had been in the Yankees' farm system since 1954, finally made it to the big team in 1961. He arrived with a reputation as an outstanding defensive outfielder with exceptional speed and would soon become known as Mantle's "caddy," frequently replacing Mickey on defense late in games. Reed, who had been an outstanding football player at the University of Mississippi and played for Ole Miss in the 1953 Sugar Bowl against Georgia Tech, would get into three games for the Yankees as a defensive replacement in the 1961 World Series. Consequently, he is one of only a handful of players to have played in both a World Series and a major college football bowl game, a list that also includes Jackie Jensen, Chuck Essegian, Deion Sanders, and Darin Erstad.

Reed's biggest moment in baseball came on Sunday, June 24, 1962, in Detroit's Tiger Stadium. With the score tied 7–7 in the 13th inning, Reed entered the game for defense. The game would go 22 innings and take seven hours to complete. It was, at the time, the longest game by time in baseball history and the longest game by innings in Yankees history. Reed batted four times in the game. In the top of the 22nd inning, he crushed a two-run homer that would give the Yankees a 9–7 victory. It was Reed's only home run in 222 major league at-bats.

"I felt fortunate to be able to get into a World Series," said Reed. "Bob Cerv had to have knee surgery, and I took his place on the roster. So that worked out good for me. I was just a rookie and I didn't get to play very much, but both Roger and Mickey were good to me.

"If I asked Roger to do something, he'd do it. He would never hesitate. There was a guy from Mississippi by the name of Fulton—'Steamboat Fulton' they called him. He was a sportswriter for a local state newspaper and he came up to New York for the 1961 World Series. I asked Roger if he would get in a picture with me, and Mantle and this guy and Roger didn't hesitate. I got along fine with Roger.

"Same with Mickey. I remember in 1987, I think it was, they had a card show in Atlantic City for the 1961 team. I got there in the afternoon and we were all signing balls. Mickey had apparently had a few drinks and we were talking and he said to me, 'Do you think you could outrun me?' I said, 'I could tonight.'

"Mickey was the greatest player I ever saw. He had the tools to do it. I just don't think he used all his tools. He didn't train like he should have. Mickey just never tried to improve his physical ability. I thought he could have been a world-class sprinter if he had tried. I think he could have done whatever he wanted.

"I had great admiration for Mantle. He amazed me. He was so strong and the things he could do. He had a magical name. When I first signed with the Yankees, I said 'Mickey Mantle move over, here I come.' I was like most kids when they sign their first contract. They think they've made it, that you can go right up there and move somebody over. After my first spring training with the Yankees, I realized something; back then a pitcher had a better chance of making the ballclub than anybody else, unless somebody retired at a position and it happened to be your position, then you might have a chance.

"I got to the point that I knew what Ralph Houk wanted me to do. Just being there was one of the best things that ever happened to me. All my life, I dreamed of playing in the big leagues, and I got to do that."

$$*$$

On May 31, Mantle and Maris homered again and the Yankees beat the Red Sox 7–6.

At this point, the newspapers were paying more attention to the dynamic duo of Mantle and Maris (the M&M

Boys in headlines) than they did to any potential assault on Babe Ruth's record. After all, despite his home run spurt, Maris was still four games off Ruth's record pace of 1927 and Mantle was only even with the Babe's pace. And there still was Ruth's safety net to consider, his defining, incredible finishing kick of 17 home runs in the month of September.

So, as May morphed into June, nobody was closely monitoring Maris' and Mantle's pace against Ruth. At least not yet they weren't. That would come later.

CHAPTER EIGHT

Crouching Tiger

JUNE GOT OFF TO A ROCKY START for the Yankees—literally. After dropping a 7–5 decision to the Red Sox in the final of a four-game series in Boston, the Yankees climbed aboard their charter for a flight to Chicago where they would engage the White Sox for three games. An hour out of Chicago's Midway Airport, the plane ran into a fierce storm that caused severe turbulence, one of those white-knuckle flights that are not for the faint of heart.

The team managed to land safely in Chicago and the next night pounded the White Sox 6–2 as Roger Maris hit his 13th home run off a pitcher from Anardarko, Oklahoma, with the colorful and mouth-filling name of Calvin Coolidge Julius Caesar Tuskahoma McLish, and Yogi Berra blasted two, his seventh and eighth. Whitey Ford went the distance to raise his record to 7–2.

In the second game of the series, Maris belted his 14th home run, a three-run shot in the top of the eighth off Bob Shaw that gave the Yankees a 5–2 lead. After a long, uphill climb, Maris had tied his teammate, Mantle, for the team and league lead in home runs. Maris' heroics were short-lived as the Sox came back with three runs of their own in the bottom of the eighth. In the bottom of the 13th inning, Roy Sievers hit what today would be called a "walk-off" home run and the Sox beat the Yankees 6–5.

The Yankees came right back the next day to dismantle the White Sox 10–1. Maris hit another home run, his 15th of the season. He had homered in three straight games, in five of the previous six games, and he had hit 12 home runs in the previous 17 games. Suddenly, writers covering the team noticed that the Yankees as a team were beginning to mount home run numbers to rival other offensive juggernauts of the past, posing a threat to several home run records. They noted that Maris' third-inning home run off Chicago's Russ Kemmerer on June 4 gave the Yankees a home run in 12 consecutive games. The major league record for home runs in consecutive games by one team was 25 by the New York Yankees in 1941.

From June 4 to June 8, the Yankees won six straight games with Maris raising his home run total to 17 in that six-game stretch. After his slow start, Maris had heated up, belting 14 home runs in the previous 21 games. The Yankees increased their home run streak to 17 games, eight short of the major league record, but were finally stopped on June 8 in the second game of a doubleheader in Kansas City.

Despite their power explosion, the Yankees were unable to climb out of third place. If Yankees hitters were benefiting from expansion that had diluted American League pitching (two new teams meant that the American League would have to provide for anywhere from 20 to 25

The Yankees' M&M Boys, Roger Maris (left) and Mickey Mantle (right), get together with Tigers' C&C Boys, Rocky Colavito (second from left) and Norm Cash (second from right), before a showdown series between the American League's two top teams in 1961. That season Maris and Mantle would combine for 115 home runs and 269 RBIs and Colavito and Cash would combine for 86 home runs and 272 RBIs. (PHOTO BY KIDWILER COLLECTION/DIAMOND IMAGES/GETTY IMAGES)

additional pitchers who, without expansion, would have been pitching in the minor leagues), so, too, were hitters on other teams also benefiting. In addition to Mantle and Maris, Norm Cash and Rocky Colavito in Detroit, Harmon Killebrew in Minnesota, and Jim Gentile in Baltimore all would hit more than 40 homers; Cash, Colavito, Gentile, Killebrew, and Bob Allison of the Twins all would drive in more than 100 runs, with Mantle, Maris, Cash, Colavito, Gentile, and Killebrew driving in 122 or more.

By contrast, in the American League the preceding season, without expansion and, granted, with eight fewer games, only Mantle hit 40 home runs, and only Maris, Minnie Minoso, Vic Wertz, and Jim Lemon drove in 100 runs or more, with only Maris topping 105.

While Maris appeared to be on a homer-a-day diet, Mantle had cooled off somewhat. He had hit only one home run in 10 games when, on June 9, he hit a three-run blast (he also singled, walked twice, and drove in four runs) in the Yankees' 8–6 win over the Athletics that would help kick start a five-game winning streak.

On June 11, the Yanks swept a pair from the Angels 2–1 and 5–1, with all seven of the Yankees' runs coming as a result of home runs. In the first game, Berra hit a pair of solo shots in the second and seventh innings. Maris had one hit, a single, in four at-bats but showed that he was more than a pretty face and a potent bat with a spectacular, leaping, game-saving catch that took a home run away from former Yankee Ken Hunt leading off the top of the seventh with the score tied 1–1.

In the second game, Mantle gave the Yanks an early lead with a three-run homer. It was his 18th of the season and it tied him again with Maris for the league lead…but not for long. Maris belted his 19th in the third inning and his 20th in the seventh.

The Yankees left home and began a 16-game trip that would take them to Cleveland, Detroit, Kansas City, Minnesota, and Los Angeles. After dropping the first game in Cleveland, they won the next two and inched ahead of the Indians and Tigers into first place by percentage points. Then it was on to Detroit for a three-game showdown series with the Tigers.

The Yankees arrived in Detroit to learn that the Tigers had shelled out a team record $100,000 bonus to sign a 19-year-old catcher named Bill Freehan, a Detroit kid who was a football and baseball star at the University of Michigan.

Freehan was an 11-time All-Star who would play his entire 15-year major league career with the Tigers. When he retired after the 1976 season, Freehan held major league records for catchers (since broken) in fielding percentage (.9333), putouts (9,941), and total chances (10,734), and he was ninth in games caught (1,581).

Frustration bubbled over for the Yanks in the first game of the series against the Tigers on June 16. The Yankees committed three errors in the first inning, two of them by Maris on one play. The Tigers took a 3–0 lead into the top of the fourth when Phil Regan retired the Yankees in order, striking Mantle out for the second time to end the inning.

The Yankees made five errors in the game in all, Maris and Mantle were both held hitless, and the Yanks fell to the Tigers 4–2 to the delight of 51,774 hostile fans in Detroit.

To add to the Tigers fans' joy, they saw Mantle strike out in his first two at-bats and, after the second strikeout, angrily fling his bat and his helmet.

By now, Mantle's public displays of frustration—tossed bats, smashed batting helmets, battered water coolers—were the stuff of legend and had been going on since his rookie season 10 years earlier. Mantle and Billy Martin were notorious for throwing things after striking out, and Casey Stengel had tried in vain to break them of the habit.

"Lookit," Stengel told them, "strikeouts are part of the game. You're going to strike out. That's okay. I don't want you to throw things or punch things. You might get hurt, or you might hurt one of your teammates. Just laugh it off when you strike out."

It seemed like a good idea to Martin, who came up with a plan that he proposed to Mantle.

"The next time you strike out, just laugh it off," Martin said. "And I'll do the same thing."

According to Mantle, that's exactly what they did. "I'd strike out and go back to the bench laughing. 'Imagine that, I struck out again. Ha, ha. Ha.'

"Billy would strike out and he'd gently put his bat and his helmet on the ground and say, 'Ha, ha, ha, how about that guy striking me out with a hanging curveball? Ha, ha. Ha.'

"This went on for a couple of days, and we could see Stengel was getting pissed. Finally, one day Billy strikes out and he comes back and he's laughing, and the Old Man just looks at him and says, 'All right, that will be enough of that shit.'"

Regan, who later in his career would become known as "The Vulture" because of his penchant for picking up cheap wins when he was a relief pitcher for the Los Angeles Dodgers, continued to baffle the Yankees into the seventh inning when Moose Skowron opened with a single but was forced in a close play at second, so close in fact it set off Ralph Houk, the Yankees' rookie manager. He stormed out of the dugout and confronted second-base umpire Joe Linsalata. In a scene that would be repeated many times over in the next few years, Houk tossed his cap on the ground and kicked dirt until he was tossed out of the game for the first (but not the last) time in his managerial career.

If Houk's histrionics were designed to motivate and awaken his slumbering athletes, he failed to achieve the desired result…at least not immediately. Mantle and Maris both went hitless against Regan, and the Yanks lost the series opener 4–2. They lost again the following night 12–10 (despite Maris' 23rd homer and Mantle's 20th), as Al Kaline drove in five runs and Norm Cash drove in three. The defeat dropped the Yankees back into third place behind Detroit and Cleveland.

Once again, as he had done many times in the past and would continue to do for the next several years, Whitey Ford was the Yankees' stopper. He pitched eight shutout innings, held the Tigers to three hits, and struck out 12, salvaging the final game of the three game series 9–0 for his 11th win of the season. Buoyed by the thought that once the game ended, the Yankees would fly by charter to Kansas City and he would be reunited with his family for the first time in six weeks, Maris belted his 24th home run.

When the Yankees arrived in Kansas City, they learned that the Athletics had announced a change in managers. Their new skipper would be Hank Bauer, who had been involved in the trade that brought Maris to the Yankees two years earlier and who had been a wildly popular Yankee and Maris' right-field predecessor. Bauer would be a player/manager. To even further extend the perception of an incestuous relationship between the Yankees and Kansas City, Bauer was taking the managerial reins from another one-time Yankee, Joe (Flash) Gordon, their second baseman in the 1930s and 40s and the 1942 American League Most Valuable Player.

In his first game as a manager, June 19, Bauer watched Maris break a 2–2 tie with a home run in the top of the ninth. But in the bottom of the ninth, Norm Siebern, another former Yankee also part of the trade for Maris, tied the score with an inside-the-park home run, and Wes Covington, pinch hitting for Leo Posada (Jorge's uncle), belted a home run off Luis Arroyo to give the A's a dramatic 4–3 win and Bauer his first victory as a manager.

In the third game of the series against the Athletics, on June 21, Mantle exploded for a three-run homer in the first, his 21st, and a two-run homer in the seventh, his 22nd, to knock in all five runs in a 5–3 victory. Not to be outdone, the following night Maris had four hits and four RBIs in an 8–3 win over the A's. Maris seemed energized by playing in his adopted hometown, in front of friends and family, and especially from his brief reunion with his wife and children. In the four-game series he had three singles, a double, a triple, three home runs, and six RBIs in 17 at-bats. The three home runs gave him 27 for the season, putting him five homers ahead of Mantle and 12 games ahead of Babe Ruth's record pace.

The countdown to a home run record was about to begin in earnest.

CHAPTER NINE

M&M

As June was drawing to a close and July beckoned, Roger Maris was at peace. He had recently spent five wonderful, relaxing days with his family at his home in Raytown, a Kansas City suburb. He no longer had negative feelings about playing in the "Big City."

With a full season behind him, Maris had adjusted to being a Yankee and playing in New York. He was comfortable in his surroundings and with his teammates. He even began spending time on the road with the team's biggest star, Mickey Mantle, and later shared an apartment in Queens with Mantle and Bob Cerv, his friend and teammate from his Kansas City days.

At first, when he arrived in New York, Maris lived in a hotel, which he found to be a lonely existence. When Cerv joined the team, Maris suggested that they share an apartment. It would give them companionship and it would be more economical. Maris' friend, Big Julie Isaacson, found them a pleasant, comfortable place just across the Triboro Bridge from the

Bronx on a quiet, tree-lined street in Queens near the Van Wyck Expressway, not far from what was then known as Idlewild (now John F. Kennedy) Airport.

It was Maris who suggested that they invite Mantle to join them. Mantle had been living in the fashionable, and exorbitant, St. Moritz Hotel on Central Park South, and Maris convinced him that he would be better off in the quiet of Queens, away from the hustle and bustle of the city with its bright lights and many temptations. It would also be cheaper.

Mantle moved into the apartment and stayed there until the final days of the 1961 season when his wife and Maris' wife came to New York. Mantle, Maris, and Cerv would drive together to Yankee Stadium in Maris' convertible. Occasionally they prepared their own meals. They would spend days off lounging at home, away from reporters, photographers, and autograph-seekers, resting, watching television, competing in a game of putting a golf ball into a cup on their living room rug.

Mantle told Robert L. Teague of the *New York Times* that he might go to a movie on the road, never at home.

"You can't have a private life," Mantle said. "It's just impossible. Everywhere you go, people think they know you."

"I like the movies, too," Maris told Teague. "But I haven't seen one all year. Hobbies? Well, none around here. When I'm home [in Raytown], I like to go bowling."

On the road, Maris roomed with third baseman Clete Boyer. Mantle, befitting his superstar status, received a single room. So did Whitey Ford. The two buddies would request adjoining rooms, and they would open the door between their rooms to make it seem as if they were occupying a suite.

Adding to Maris' enjoyment was the fact that he was now with a team that was winning consistently and was a perennial pennant contender. Playing in meaningful games got his competitive juices flowing and making an important contribution to his team's success exhilarated him. He even introduced a new phrase into the baseball lexicon, a word to describe a home run. He called it a "Tonk."

Why "Tonk?"

"You know," Maris explained, "when you hit a ball good, it goes 'Tonk.'"

How do you spell *Tonk*? Curious reporters wanted to know.

"Damned if I know how to spell it," Maris said. "It's just Tonk."

The magnitude of the chase of Babe Ruth's home run record still had not kicked in. The hordes of media that would eventually follow Yankees games and report on the home run race had not yet begun to arrive. No one, including Maris himself, was taking the challenge to Babe Ruth's single-season home run record seriously. Maris had not yet begun to sense the pressure of challenging Babe's precious record. Or had he?

For seven games, from June 23 to June 30, Maris failed to hit a home run, stuck on 27 as Mantle inched up to 25. Mantle's latest was an inside-the-park home run on June 30 in a 5–1 win over the Washington Senators at Yankee Stadium.

Whitey Ford went the distance in a brisk 1:56, allowing five hits and striking out eight for his 14th win of the season. It also was his eighth victory in the month of June, the most wins in a month by a left-hander in American League history (in the National League, Rube Marquard of the New York Giants won eight games in a month in 1912). The last pitcher, lefty or righty, to win eight games in a month had been Lynwood "Schoolboy" Rowe of the Detroit Tigers in July 1934.

Mantle's home run came in the bottom of the sixth with two outs and the score tied 1–1. The ball hit against the center-field wall just to the right of the 461' sign, and Mantle, with his blazing speed, circled the bases and scored without a slide.

"I'd rather hit 'em out," Mantle said. "It doesn't seem like a homer when you have to run."

By July 1, the home run race between teammates Maris and Mantle, the Yankees' M&M Boys, and against Babe Ruth's record of 60 homers in 1927, had picked up steam. It was the big story in baseball throughout the major leagues.

Could they do it? Would they do it? Would both of them do it? If only one of them was going to do it, which would it be?

*

The home run race and the attention devoted to the M&M Boys spiked sales in M&M candy, but Maris and Mantle did not share in any of the profits.

An exotic dancer in Las Vegas billed herself as Mickey Maris.

Several newspapers around the country, in an effort to boost circulation, sponsored contests in which readers

The M&M Boys, Mickey Mantle, left, and Roger Maris, pose for a portrait at Yankee Stadium in 1961, the year of the home run chase.
(Photo by C&G Collections/Getty Images)

were asked to predict how many home runs Maris and Mantle would hit and offered prizes to the winners. One such contest appeared in *The Miami News* and caught the attention of a freshman baseball player at Florida State University, who submitted his entry.

The player's name was Woody Woodward. He was a cousin of actress Joanne Woodward, and he would play nine seasons in the major leagues with the Milwaukee/Atlanta Braves and Cincinnati Reds. He was a member of the Reds' 1970 National League championship team. Later, he served as general manager of the New York Yankees, Philadelphia Phillies, and Seattle Mariners.

"I filled out the ballot and said I thought Roger would hit 61 and Mickey 54," said Woodward. "You also had to give a reason for your answer, and I said it was because Roger was a left-handed hitter, best suited for Yankee Stadium. I got $50."

＊

On July 1, in the second inning, Mantle crushed his 26th home run, batting right-handed into the left-field bleachers to the left of the 457' sign. It was the 1,000th RBI of his career. In the third, Mantle again hit one into the left-field bleachers for his 27th home run to tie Maris for the league lead. But not for long.

Dale Long, a former and future Yankee, had given the Senators a 6–5 lead with a home run leading off the top of the ninth. In the bottom of the ninth, Tony Kubek singled and Maris ended his home run drought and regained the American League home run lead from Mantle with No. 28, a game-winning blast into the right-field seats. It came off Dave Sisler, the youngest son of the great Hall of Famer George Sisler, whose career was highlighted by two spectacular achievements. The elder Sisler's 257 hits in 1920 stood as the major league record for 84 years until it was broken by Ichiro Suzuki of the Seattle Mariners, who collected 262 hits in 2004 in a 162-game schedule. And Sisler's 41-game hitting streak in 1922 was baseball's modern record for 19 years until Joe DiMaggio hit safely in 56 consecutive games in 1941.

On July 2, the Yankees hit five home runs and buried the Senators 13–4. Maris drilled a pair, his 29th and 30th, putting him eight games ahead of Ruth's pace. Mantle was walked in each of his first four times at bat (he would walk 126 times in the 1961 season, nine of the walks intentional: batting in front of Mantle for the most part, Maris walked 94 times, none intentional). In his final at-bat in the eighth inning, Mantle kept his hitting streak alive at 15 games with his 28th home run. He was four games ahead of Ruth.

The Fourth of July holiday produced a whopping crowd of 74,246 (not a record: the Yankees drew 81,841 for a doubleheader against the Red Sox on May 30, 1938, before the fire department put a safety requirement limit on the number of spectators allowed in public buildings).

The Tigers arrived in New York with a record of 49–27 and a one-game lead over the Yankees, who were 47–27. So evenly matched were the two teams that in their first nine meetings of the season, the Yanks had won five games, the Tigers four.

In the first game of the holiday doubleheader, Whitey Ford was dominant. He pitched a complete game five-hitter and struck out 11 for a 6–2 victory. It was Ford's ninth straight victory, and it raised his season record to a stunning 15–2. The Yankees exploded for all their runs off Don Mossi in the sixth inning and moved ahead of the Tigers into first place by .0037. But their position at the top of the heap in the American League was only temporary. Some four hours later, the Tigers were back in first place following a heart-stopping 4–3 victory in 10 innings.

The Yankees trailed 2–0 in the eighth inning when, with two outs, Tony Kubek doubled and Maris followed with his 31st home run to tie the score, right fielder Al Kaline making a courageous but futile dive over the 4' fence into the right-field seats.

In the top of the ninth, the Tigers loaded the bases with two outs, with Cuban native Chico Fernandez on third base as a pinch-runner. With home run slugger Rocky Colavito at bat, the Tigers daringly attempted a triple steal, Fernandez sliding home under the tag of catcher John Blanchard to put the Tigers up 3–2. Later, Fernandez joked that if he hadn't slid home safely, he would have been sent back to Cuba for a tractor—a reference to Cuban dictator Fidel Castro's offer to return prisoners from the Bay of Pigs invasion to the United States in exchange for 500 large farm tractors.

The Yankees again tied the score with a run in the bottom of the ninth, but in the top of the 10th, the Tigers once again showed their daring. With two outs, they had runners on second and third and their pitcher, Frank Lary, at bat. With two strikes on him, Lary surprised the overflow crowd and the Yankees by dropping a bunt along the third-base line. Pitcher Bill Stafford bounded off the mound, fielded the ball, and flipped to catcher Blanchard, but Steve Boros slid home safely.

When Kubek opened the bottom of the tenth with a single, Tigers manager Bob Scheffing went to his bullpen. Lefthander Hank Aguirre retired Maris and Yogi Berra, then right-hander Terry Fox got Moose Skowron for the final out and the Tigers, with a 4–3 victory, were back in first place.

Lary, a renowned Yankee killer, was the winning pitcher, his third victory of the season over the Yanks, raising his career record against them to a remarkable 26–9.

The Yankees would then win five straight games over the Indians and Red Sox to regain first place. But their hold on the league lead was brief. On Sunday, July 9, in the final game before the year's first All-Star game (Major League Baseball experimented with two All-Star games in 1959–62) the Yankees lost the second game of a doubleheader to the Red Sox and fell back into second place, a half game behind the Tigers. Maris reached the break with 33 homers, 13 games ahead of Ruth. Mantle had 29 homers and was two games behind Ruth.

*

In a vote of players, coaches, and managers, the Yankees placed three starters on the All-Star team, Roger Maris in right field, Mickey Mantle in center, and Tony Kubek at shortstop. First baseman Norm Cash of the Tigers led all American League vote-getters with 235. Maris polled 233 votes and Mantle 230. Whitey Ford was chosen as the American League's starting pitcher. Two other Yankees, Yogi Berra and Elston Howard, were picked as extra players.

After the doubleheader with the Red Sox, Mantle and Ford flew to San Francisco where they planned to spend the day before the All-Star Game playing golf. When they arrived in San Francisco, Ford telephoned his friend, New York restaurateur Toots Shor, who had flown out for the game, and asked him if he knew anyone that had a golf membership where he and Mantle could play. Shor did: his friend Horace Stoneham, owner of the Giants.

Arrangements were made at the Olympic Club, but when Ford and Mantle got there, they realized they had no clubs, no golf shoes, and no golf gloves. So they went to the pro shop, bought alpaca sweaters, gloves, and shoes and rented clubs. The cost was $400, but the club would not take cash, so they charged the amount to Stoneham's account and figured they'd settle up with him later that night.

When Ford tried to reimburse Stoneham the $400, he refused to take it.

"I'll tell you what," he told Ford. "Double or nothing! If you get Willie [Mays] out tomorrow, you don't owe me a thing. If Willie gets a hit, you owe me $800."

Ford accepted the challenge, but when he told Mantle about Stoneham's deal, Mickey went berserk.

"You against Mays!" he said. "Are you crazy?"

Ford picked up the rest of the story.

"I got the first two batters out in the first inning, and now here comes Willie. I really didn't know how to pitch the guy because everything I threw up there he hit and hit hard. I threw him two curveballs, and he hit both of them foul about 500' down the left-field line. Now I had him 0–2, and all I could think about was Mickey in center field, worrying about the $800.00.

"I never had much luck throwing the spitball, although I had been experimenting with it on the sidelines and occasionally in a game. I never knew where it was going to go, but if I ever was going to throw one, this was the perfect time. I figured I might as well try something different. I had nothing to lose. He was hitting everything I threw up there anyway.

"I loaded one up and threw it. The ball was heading right at Willie, between his shoulder and his elbow. Willie thought it was going to hit him, so he jumped out of the way, and damned if the ball doesn't drop down and sail right over the plate.

"'Strike three,' shouted the home-plate umpire, Stan Landes.

"There were 70 million people watching the game on television. It was only an exhibition game, but 70 million people saw our famous center fielder jumping up and down and clapping his hands as he ran in from center field.

"Mays saw this and he looked at me with a funny expression. As we passed each other, Willie said, 'What's that crazy bastard clapping for?'

"Willie must have thought Mickey was clapping because of the so-called rivalry between them, and the fans probably thought the same thing. But that was not it at all. There was no rivalry between Mickey and Willie. They liked and respected one another. Mickey was clapping because we had just saved ourselves $800."

*

With Casey Stengel "retired," Paul Richards, whose Baltimore Orioles finished second to the Yankees in 1960, was selected to manage the American League squad in the All-Star Game. Richards ignored Houk's batting order and batted Mantle third and Maris fourth, but neither of the two Yankees sluggers excelled at bat as the National League beat the American League 5–4 in 10 innings. Mantle struck out twice, grounded out, and was replaced by Al Kaline. Maris played the entire game, batted five times, struck out twice, grounded out, walked, and singled against Sandy Koufax.

The game was played in San Francisco's Candlestick Park and is best remembered for the powerful gust of wind that literally blew National League pitcher Stu Miller of the Giants off of the mound. The second All-Star Game, played in Boston's Fenway Park on July 31, ended in a 1–1 tie when the game was called in the ninth inning because of rain. It would be the only All-Star Game tie until 2002.

Because of a strained hamstring, Maris didn't start but he appeared as a pinch-hitter for John Romano and popped out to the second baseman. Again, Mantle was hitless in three at-bats. He didn't bat against Stu Miller in the first All-Star Game but did in the second. He came to bat in the ninth inning and struck out.

"They warned me about his curveball," Mantle said, "but I never expected a curve that slow. I felt like I waited an hour before I swung at one, but I was still way out in front."

Only another pitcher could appreciate Miller, and Whitey Ford jumped on the bandwagon.

"It was a treat to watch him," Ford said. "I had a good look at him from the bullpen and I noticed how he would sort of twitch his shoulder and move his head to the side before he threw a pitch. Mantle told me it was the best head fake he ever saw."

∗

The Yankees resumed the season and Maris and Mantle resumed hitting home runs on July 13 in Chicago. The Yanks struck early against Early Wynn, who was trying for the 292nd win of an illustrious career. Bobby Richardson led off with a single and moved to second on a sacrifice bunt by Tony Kubek. Maris and Mantle then connected for back-to-back homers. Maris reached the upper deck in right for his 34th of the season. Mantle hit one into the upper deck in center field for his 30th of the season and the 350th of his career. The Yankees coasted to a 6–2 victory and moved back into first place ahead of the Tigers by percentage points.

Mantle homered again the following night, but that was the extent of the Yankees' offense against Juan Pizarro, who stifled the Yanks on seven hits in a 6–1 defeat. But the Tigers also lost, so the Yankees remained in first place.

In the final game of the three-game series, the Yankees found themselves down by six runs after four innings but came back to win 9–8 in 10 innings. Maris had a spectacular game both offensively and defensively. In the third inning, he belted his 35th home run. In the sixth, he hit a triple that he might have tried to stretch into an inside-the-park home run, but leading off the inning, Maris wisely played it safe and held up at third. In the ninth, he doubled home the tying run, leaving him without a single that would have completed the cycle.

In the field, Maris threw out J.C. Martin attempting to stretch a single into a double in the second, and in the eighth, he shot down Luis Aparicio trying to score from third on a fly ball by Jim Landis.

The Yankees moved on to Baltimore where they were scheduled for three games, a single game on Sunday, July 16, and a make-up doubleheader on Monday night, July 17, the second game a replay of the 5–5 tie of April 22.

Bud Daley pitched the Yankees to a 2–1 victory with a four-hitter in the first game. Mantle knocked in both runs with his 32nd home run in the fourth and an RBI double in the ninth.

Before the Monday doubleheader, manager Ralph Houk fulfilled a commitment to speak at a luncheon meeting of the Baltimore Sports Reporters Association, where he was asked if he thought Mantle or Maris would break Ruth's home run record.

"I hope they both break the record," Houk said. "That would make me look like a better manager. But our job is to win pennants, not worry about setting individual records."

Houk did say that if the Yankees clinched the pennant and Mantle and Maris were still in the hunt for the record, he would alter his lineup to bat Maris first and Mantle second to give them additional at-bats. But Houk never did alter his lineup. Mantle, when he played, remained in the No. 4 spot and Maris stayed in the No. 3 hole except when Mantle was out of the lineup and he batted fourth.

*

While Houk was speaking to the Baltimore sports reporters and commissioner Ford C. Frick was preparing for a meeting with a group of baseball writers in the commissioner's New York offices in Rockefeller Center, word came out of Atlanta that Ty Cobb had died in Emory University Hospital at the age of 74. Mickey Cochrane, Ray Schalk, and Nap Rucker would be the only former major league players to attend his funeral.

Asked to comment on Cobb's passing, Frick lauded the "Georgia Peach" as "a great baseball player who was representative of a competitive spirit that must be continued if baseball is to continue."

Frick said the death of Cobb "marks the passage of one of the few remaining links between the old and the new. We have many baseball players, but very few Ty Cobbs. He belongs with the Ruths, Mathewsons, Alexanders, and Johnsons of a golden era."

Casey Stengel called Cobb "the most sensational of all the players I have seen in all my life. By sensational I mean he surprised all his opponents. He would shock them with startling base-running plays and he could always outhit any opponent, even if they were great players."

Stengel said he once saw Cobb tag up from third and score on an infield pop-up. "He just waited until the fielder got ready to throw to the pitcher," Stengel said.

George Weiss said, "There's no denying that Cobb stood alone as a baseball player, undoubtedly the greatest of all."

And Roy Hamey added, "Ty Cobb, of course, was a legend in American sports. His feats were such that nobody has seriously challenged his immortal records."

Coincidentally, Cobb was among old-time players who branded Maris as unworthy to replace Babe Ruth in the record books and who appealed to Commissioner Frick to find a way to retain Ruth's name on the books as baseball's all-time single-season home run king.

The irony was that Cobb and Ruth had waged a long-time rivalry—each with avid supporters—to the claim of "Baseball's Greatest Player" and that Cobb often showed his disdain for Ruth's penchant for home runs. He believed that the science of hitting required a greater skill than the mere brute strength of hitting a baseball over distant fences.

Cobb had actually led the American League in home runs in 1909 with nine, all of them inside the park. He was more interested in raising his batting average than in padding his home run total, which is reflected in his record lifetime average of .366 and his record 11 batting titles but only 117 home runs in 11,434 at-bats.

Things changed when Babe Ruth came along in the 1920s and started grabbing headlines and capturing the attention and adulation of fans with his prodigious home runs. Those Ruthian blasts were fan magnets because their like had never been seen before—which was precisely how Cobb purported to view Ruth and his home runs, as fads with no staying power.

Proud and egotistical, Cobb was envious of Ruth's popularity. He openly condemned Ruth's batting style. The more home runs the Babe hit, the more popular he grew, and the more popular he became, the more hostile toward him Cobb became.

"Anybody can hit home runs if he wants to," Cobb said.

Early in the 1925 season, at the age of 38, Cobb decided the time had come to prove his point. Envious of the attention the boisterous, braggadocios Babe was getting with his home runs, Cobb told a reporter that for the first time he was going to swing for the fences.

In two games in St. Louis, on May 5–6, Cobb came to bat 12 times, had nine hits, hit five home runs, accumulated 24 total bases, and drove in 11 runs. Having proved his point, Cobb went back to his preferred style of hitting. He hit only seven more home runs for the rest of the season and batted .378.

The question is if Cobb so despised Ruth and disapproved of his style of hitting, why, some 36 years later, did he come to the Babe's defense by disparaging Maris in the controversy over the single-season home run record? The simple answer is that it was not so much that Cobb was favoring Ruth over Maris, but that he was favoring baseball of his era over that of the current era.

Later that day, Mantle was asked to comment on Cobb's passing.

"I'm sorry to hear it," he said. "He used to come see me in the dugout when he visited New York and give me some batting tips. He would say, 'Come here, kid, let me show you what you're doing wrong.' He would tell me I was standing too close to the plate or too far away. He must have helped me two or three times."

Roger Maris had no comment.

Chapter Ten

*

THERE WAS NO ASTERISK. Not then. Not now. Not ever.

The myth that an asterisk was used to denote that Roger Maris needed expansion and a longer schedule of games to exceed Babe Ruth's single-season home run record has been perpetuated in story and on film. But it's not true. It never was. There never was an asterisk. What there was for almost 50 years, however, were two entries in baseball's official record books, as such:

Most Home Runs, Season
61 Roger E. Maris, AL: N.Y. 1961 (162 G/S)
60 George H. Ruth, AL: N.Y. 1927

So, there was no asterisk on the books, in fact, but there was an asterisk in the minds of baseball fans, and it would remain there forever.

The whole asterisk controversy was born on July 17, 1961. A preview of what was to come on that day was touched on by veteran baseball writer Dan Daniel in his column in *The*

Sporting News, a column that, viewed in retrospect, was clairvoyant.

"Commissioner Ford Frick will soon call a conference with the Records Committee of the Baseball Writers' Association of America," Daniel wrote. "The commissioner is quite aroused over the chance that the new 162-game schedule, eight more games than ever before, will produce records.

"Suppose Roger Maris hits 61 with the help of those extra contests? Suppose after 154 games, Maris has 58 or 59 homers, then totals 61 over the rest of the season? Frick believes it would not be right to recognize the mark after 154 games. The commissioner has strong backing in this attitude. If Ruth had gone to 162 games, he would have hit seven more homers if he had continued at his current pace. In the last eight games of 1927, Babe hit seven."

Apprised of Daniel's column, Maris said, "How could anyone know that Ruth would have hit seven more home runs if he had played 162 games? He could have hit a couple more, or maybe none. I don't know how many he would have hit, and neither does anyone else."

On July 17, baseball commissioner Ford C. Frick was meeting with a group of veteran baseball writers at the commissioner's office in Rockefeller Center. (Coincidentally, the meeting came on the very day that Ty Cobb, one of Roger Maris' most severe critics, had passed away.) Frick was ready with a prepared statement which he read to the assembled media:

"Any player who may hit more than 60 home runs during his club's first 154 games would be recognized as having established a new record. However, if the player does not hit more than 60 until after his club has played 154 games, there would have to be some distinctive mark in the record books to show that Babe Ruth's record was set under a 154-game schedule and the total of more than 60 was compiled while a 162-game schedule was in effect.

"We also would apply the same reasoning if a player should equal Ruth's total of 60 in the first 154 games, he would be recognized as tying Ruth's record. If in more than 154 games, there would be a distinction in the record books."

Frick's statement would raise more questions than it answered.

- Why was there no mention of the fact that, when Ruth hit his record 60 home runs in 1927, the Yankees played 155 games because of an early season tie?

- Why was there nothing said about other single-season records—George Sisler's 257 hits, Earl Webb's 67 doubles, Chief Wilson's 36 triples, Hack Wilson's 191 RBIs, Ty Cobb's 96 stolen bases, Jack Chesbro's 41 wins and 48 complete games, Rube Waddell's 349 strikeouts, Grover Cleveland Alexander's 16 shutouts?

At the time of the meeting, the focus seemed to be not on Maris but on his teammate, Mantle, who, although he was three home runs behind Maris, was deemed more likely to break the record. Also present at the meeting was an undercurrent of suspicion for the true motives of Frick. It was well known among the writers that the commissioner, once a baseball writer himself, had served as Ruth's ghostwriter and had remained a close friend of the Babe's who visited Ruth on his deathbed in New York Memorial Hospital. The writers were convinced that the singular purpose of Frick's statement was not for the protection of the sanctity of baseball's record but to sustain Ruth's legacy.

At one point, during a question and answer session with the commissioner, when Frick used the phrase "some distinctive mark," Dick Young, the longtime baseball writer and columnist for the *New York Daily News,* who had acquired the reputation of being the "conscience of baseball," said, "You mean like an asterisk?"

Frick was said to have replied, "Yes." But even though the commissioner never uttered the word "asterisk," a phrase, and a controversy, had begun.

Frick's statement brought an avalanche of comments from people in all walks of life, not only baseball, and there were arguments on both sides of the issue.

A poll of members of the Baseball Writers' Association of America revealed that those who covered baseball for the country's major daily newspapers sided with the commissioner's ruling by a vote of 2-to-1.

Yankees manager Ralph Houk said he planned to send a wire to Frick if the Yankees were in first place after 154 games, at which point he would tell the commissioner, "that's the pennant so far as we're concerned."

Perhaps the wisest comment of all was a question posed by no less an authority than Lawrence Peter Berra.

"What happens if one guy breaks the record inside 154 games, but the other guy ends up with more home runs after 162 games?" asked Yogi. "Then who has the record?"

In 1991, 13 years after Frick's death, then-commissioner Fay Vincent succeeded in removing the entry in the record books that acknowledged both Maris' 61 home runs in a 162-game schedule and Ruth's 60 home runs in a 154-game schedule and replaced it with one entry to make Maris the undisputed record holder.

In later years, Frank Slocum, Frick's longtime loyal chief assistant, said his boss agonized over the perception that he was motivated to protect and perpetuate the legend of his friend Ruth by giving Maris short shrift.

"It bothered him in the sense he felt people would think he would compromise something against another ballplayer to Ruth's advantage," said Slocum.

At the same time, Slocum acknowledged that he was aware how disturbed Maris was with Frick's decision.

"Early in the 1962 season, I was talking with Roger in the Yankees clubhouse and he said to me, 'Your boss screwed me around,'" said Slocum. "I said, 'Roger, let me ask you a question. Suppose there was even more expansion and the schedule goes to 170 games. Let's suppose that a guy comes along and hits his 62nd home run in the 165th game. Did he break your record?' He looked at me, grinned, and said, 'No.'"

While Frick was in New York meeting with members of the press, the Yankees and Orioles were getting ready to take the field in the first game of a twi-night doubleheader in Baltimore. Reporters cornered Maris, told him of Frick's ruling, and solicited a comment from the Yankees right fielder.

Typically, Maris evaded the issue and said all the right things—he didn't make the rules; it wasn't going to matter because breaking the home run record was merely a pipe dream; he wasn't interested in breaking records; he was interested only in helping the Yankees win the pennant.

But Maris could not resist one last comment about the commissioner's ruling.

"A season is a season," he said pointedly.

$*$

In the third inning of the first game, Memorial Stadium was pelted with a rainstorm as Whitey Ford was handcuffing Orioles batters on six hits for a 5–0 victory, his 17th of the season and 11th straight. In the sixth inning, just before the rain stopped, Mantle hit his 33rd home run, his fourth in five games, and was now only two behind Maris.

It rained again between games but stopped just as the second game was scheduled to start. The Yankees had taken a 4–1 lead in the fifth inning when the heavens opened again over Memorial Stadium with a fierce rainstorm complete with thunder and lightning. After waiting 65 minutes, the umpires concluded that the game could not be resumed and it was called. Not only did the Yankees lose what appeared to be a certain victory, washed out were Maris' 36th homer and Mantle's 34th. The game would be made up from the start as part of a doubleheader on September 19.

How ironic that on the very day Frick made his pronouncement regarding a player having to hit 61 home runs within a 154-game span in order to be considered having broken the record, both serious challengers to the record, Mantle and Maris, hit home runs that would not count. It was as if the baseball gods were doing their utmost to protect Ruth's record.

From Baltimore, the Yankees moved to Washington, D.C., for a three-game series with the floundering expansion Senators. Prior to the opening game on the night of July 18, Mantle took part in a home run–hitting contest. Three batters from each team competed in the contest, each one partnered with a member of Congress. Mantle's partner was Rep. Edwin B. Dooley, a Republican from Mamaroneck, N.Y., who years later would serve as chairman of the New York State Athletic Commission.

Mantle, who had been on a batting tear, carried his hot bat into the contest, putting on a show by driving three balls into the distant left-field bleachers that elicited "oohs" and "aahs" from the crowd as well as the lawmen. One of Mantle's drives hit at the base of a light tower atop the left-field bleachers and bounced over the wall. The blow was in the approximate location of Mantle's monster home run in 1953 off Chuck Stobbs that was measured at 565' and is the only ball ever hit to left field that sailed out of Griffith Stadium.

As winner of the home run–hitting contest, Mantle was awarded a $100 United States savings bond. His partner, Rep. Dooley, won a season pass to Senators home games.

Having warmed up with his pregame explosion, Mantle carried his hot bat into the game. In the first inning, with Bobby Richardson on base, he golfed a towering drive left-handed against Joe McClain that hit high on the light pole on the right-field fence and bounced back on the field for a two-run homer.

After striking out in his next two at-bats, Mantle faced McClain again in the eighth with two outs, nobody on base, and the score tied 3–3. The count went to 3–2. Mantle fouled off one pitch and then sent the next one soaring over the right-field scoreboard to put the Yankees ahead to stay. It was Mantle's 35th home run of the season, his sixth in six days, and it tied him with Maris, his teammate and comrade in arms. The M&M Boys were now both 17 games ahead of Ruth's record home run pace and somebody noted that the 70 home runs between them made Mantle and Maris serious threats to the record for most home runs in a season by teammates, 107 by Ruth (60) and Lou Gehrig (47) for the Yankees in 1927.

The following day, the Yankees dropped a doubleheader to the lowly Senators 8–4 and 12–2. The pressure seemed to be affecting Maris, who was hitless in the doubleheader and stretched his hitless streak to 19 at-bats over six games during which his batting average dived 17 points, from .289 to .272. Mantle, meanwhile, crushed his 36th home run in the sixth inning of the second game and moved ahead of Maris in the home run race for the first time since June 2, a portent, most observers predicted, of Mantle carrying on to challenge Ruth while Maris faded to also-ran status.

On July 21 in Boston, Maris ended a homerless drought of five games and moved back into a tie with Mantle for the home run lead by blasting his 36th off Bill Monbouquette in the first inning. The tie lasted only a matter of minutes as Mantle followed with his 37th. It was the third time that season the M&M Boys went back-to-back (they would do it only one more time). But the big home run heroics were left to John Blanchard, one of three Yankees catchers who would combine for a season total of 64 homers (Yogi Berra hit 22; Elston Howard and Blanchard hit 21 each). On this night, Blanchard belted a pinch-hit grand slam in the ninth inning to lift the Yankees to an 11–8 victory over the Red Sox.

The following night, manager Houk tried to make lightning strike twice by again calling on Blanchard as a pinch-hitter in the ninth inning. And with the Yankees trailing 9–8 once again Blanchard delivered and, in so doing, joined a long list of major league players who had hit pinch-hit home runs in consecutive times at bat.

When the Red Sox salvaged the final game of the three-game series with a 5–4 victory, the Yankees, despite having won six out of their last nine, dropped into second place in the American League, a half-game behind the Tigers.

The Yankees returned home on July 24 to face the *San Francisco* Giants, the prodigal team returning for a much-anticipated exhibition game for the benefit of sandlot baseball—which had been a ballyhooed annual event when the Giants and Dodgers were still in New York.

What made this game significant was not only the return of the beloved Giants but also a chance to see baseball's two greatest center fielders (and two of the greatest of all time) on the same field. That extravaganza brought out a crowd of 47,346, made up mostly of Giants fans. The enormous crowd led cynics to comment that the Giants would still be in New York if they had drawn a few crowds like that in the Polo Grounds (in their final year in New York, the Giants' attendance was 653,923—or 9,616 per opening, last in the National League).

The crowd was disappointed when an early downpour forced cancellation of a scheduled home run–hitting contest that would have matched Mantle, Maris, and company against the likes of Willie Mays, Orlando Cepeda, and Willie McCovey.

Which of the two center fielders, Mantle or Mays, had the upper hand in the game, won by the Giants 4–1 depends on your point of view, or more likely, on your rooting interest. In the bottom of the second inning, Mantle hit a tremendous tape-measure home run, a 450' blast off Bob Bolin into the bleachers in right-center field. In the next half inning, Mays made a bid to match Mantle. With two outs and the bases loaded, he hit a screaming line drive to the gap in right-center. But taking a page from the book of his exciting counterpart, Mantle was off with the crack of the bat. With his blazing speed, he reached the ball and caught it in his outstretched glove hand.

Mays would get his satisfaction with a two-run single in the fifth, and then, removed for a pinch runner, he left the field to an ear-splitting ovation that rocked the huge stadium.

The next night, the Yankees faced the White Sox in a twi-night doubleheader and treated a crowd of 46,240 to a frightening display of longball hitting. They bombed eight home runs in the doubleheader—four of them by Roger Maris, two in each game, good for eight RBIs; two by Clete Boyer; and one each for Mickey Mantle and Elston Howard—in a 5–1, 12–0 sweep that returned the Yankees to first place, a half game ahead of Detroit.

In one day Maris, who had hit only four home runs in his previous 16 games, had jumped back into the major league home run lead and into the conversation regarding a challenge to Babe Ruth's record. He now had 40 home runs, one more than he hit in the 1960 season, and was 24 games ahead of Ruth's 1927 pace.

Maris failed to hit a home run the following day, but the Yankees continued the barrage with four more in a 5–2 defeat of the White Sox. Boyer hit one, Mantle banged his 39th, and Blanchard tied another major league record by hitting home runs in his first two at-bats to give him home runs in four consecutive at-bats.

With Maris and Mantle separated by one home run, Maris at 40 and Mantle at 39, the *New York Times* dipped into its archives to report, "Thirty-four years ago today, a Yankee home run derby was in progress that was every bit as hot as that between Roger Maris and Mickey Mantle. That year Babe Ruth established his record of 60 homers for a 154-game season.

"Ruth and Lou Gehrig were the principals. After the Yankees beat the Browns in a doubleheader on July 26, 1927, the home run standing was Ruth 33, Gehrig 32."

Here's what Richards Vidmer wrote in the *New York Times:*

"The Great American Home Run Derby was on apace, and what a pace! The Babe clouted two home runs into the right-field bleachers in the first game, giving him 33 for the season so far, and the Buster [Gehrig] boomed one into the same section in the second which was his 32nd.

"The main interest centered on the Great Home Run Handicap between the twin thrillers, the Babe and the Buster. They alone were worth the price of admission."

*

The home run explosion in the American League in 1961, which transcended even the challenge to Babe Ruth's single-season record, led to wild speculation in an attempt to explain the cause. Everyone seemed to have a theory to explain the sudden power surge, from the dilution of pitching due to expansion, to the use of lighter bats with thinner handles, to conjecture that the baseballs used had somehow been juiced up, a charge that the manufacturer of baseballs vehemently denied.

Said Edwin J. Parker, president of Spalding, which had been supplying the major leagues with baseballs since the game began: "As far as the actual ball is concerned, it's undergone no changes in construction since 1926 when we changed from a cork to a rubber cork center. Understand that the specifications for the balls are made by the major leagues, not by us. Spalding has improved all its equipment except the absolutely unchanged major league baseball."

There were similar denials by Spalding after Ruth had raised the home run record from 27 to 29 and then to 54 and 59. In 1925, the president of Spalding and the president of the American League said that the baseball used in the major leagues that year was the same as the one used in 1910. The Babe said, "The ball is all right. It's the same as 10 years ago. It's the batters who are different. You see very few hit-and-run batters these days."

Commissioner Frick and National League president Warren Giles concurred that there was no change in the official major league baseball, but White Sox manager Al Lopez, having recently witnessed Maris hit four home runs against his team in a doubleheader, begged to differ.

"I don't care what the manufacturer says," opined the highly respected Lopez, in his day one of baseball's most erudite figures. "The ball today is even livelier than it was last season."

On the other hand, Zack Wheat, a .375 hitter for the 1924 Brooklyn Dodgers, and Stan (The Man) Musial of the St. Louis Cardinals, a seven-time National League batting champion, put the onus on the bat, not the baseball.

"In my day, we used heavy, thick-handled bats and went for hits, not homers," said Wheat.

According to Musial, "Hitters got the idea that the speed of the bat at the moment of contact was the key to long-distance hitting. So they all grabbed long, light bats with skinny handles. If they hit the ball on the heavy part it goes. But hit it on the handle and you get nothing. That explains why a .250 hitter can hit 20 homers."

Casey Stengel and baseball's last .400 hitter, Ted Williams, now retired, lined up in the "blame it on the dilution of pitching" camp.

"The pitching has thinned out," Williams said. "Expansion has reduced the caliber of major league pitchers in the American League by 20 percent. I don't want to take anything away from Roger Maris and Mickey Mantle. They're both great hitters, but they're batting against guys they never would have seen in previous years."

Supporting Williams' theory were statistics from the American League in 1960, the year before expansion, and 1961, the year of expansion. In 1960, there were 1,086 home runs hit in the eight-team American League, an average of 136 home runs per team. In 1961, there were 1,534 home runs hit in the 10-team American League, or 153 per team.

However, note that while the home run numbers jumped markedly in the American League from 1960 to 1961, which many attributed to the dilution of pitching because of expansion, at the same time home runs also increased in the National League where there was no expansion. In 1960, the eight-team National League hit 1,042 home runs, or 130 per team. In 1961, the National League, still an eight-team league, hit 1,196 home runs, or 150 per team.

Another viewpoint was that owners decided that what fans wanted was more offense in the game so they complied by bringing in the fences. The result was the Los Angeles Coliseum with its 250' left-field fence, Fenway Park with its Green Monster, Wrigley Field in Los Angeles with distances of 345' in the power alleys and Minnesota's bandbox of a ballpark, Metropolitan Stadium.

Dodgers coach Leo Durocher, for one, pointed out that the inequity of some ballparks is responsible for his team playing better on the road than it does at home.

"We have the pitching," Durocher said, "but our park is not a fair test. Playing 77 games there has to hurt our staff."

Said Yankees manager Ralph Houk: "Our guys can hit homers anywhere. But when we play in L.A.'s Wrigley Field, one of those little guys hits one 350' and it's just as good as our 450' shots."

CHAPTER ELEVEN

Stadium Bunting

I TOOK OVER AS YANKEES BEAT WRITER for the now-defunct *New York World-Telegram and Sun* on August 2, with the Yankees scheduled to play a doubleheader at Yankee Stadium against the Kansas City Athletics. I picked up the team in time to watch Mickey Mantle drill his 40th home run. It came in the first inning of the second game of a 6–5, 12–5 doubleheader sweep by the Yankees, and it moved Mantle back into a tie with Roger Maris for the major league home run lead.

The home run race had begun to heat up, attracting fans in droves and an increasing number of members of the media. Also heating up was the controversy over commissioner Ford Frick's "asterisk," the debate over whether the baseball had been souped up, and the worthiness of Maris—and to a lesser extent, Mantle—to occupy a place once inhabited by the mighty Babe Ruth.

I had covered the Yankees sporadically—mostly home games—since the 1959 season, but now I would be with them on a daily basis, home and away, and that proximity would give me insight into the various personalities.

I found Mantle to be an enigma. He could be gracious, charming, affable, cooperative, and humorous one day and rude, crude, lewd, standoffish, and irritable the next. Years later, after Mantle had retired and I had matured and gotten to know him better, I had different views of his frequent boorishness as a player. Where at the time I passed it off as rudeness, pure and simple, I later came to the conclusion that in those days he so often was in such severe pain it affected his demeanor. Still later I came to believe that the reason he was such a difficult interview was that he was so humble that he found it difficult talking about himself.

I observed that in general Mantle was respectful, helpful, and readily accessible to the older members of the writing corps, those with whom he had a history and who had earned his trust. I wondered how long it would take me to achieve that status with him. Maybe never!

Maris was different. At first, I found him to be Jolly Roger, mostly cordial, cooperative, approachable, and relatively at ease. At the same time, he spoke in a dull monotone, with platitudes and clichés. He had very little to offer, but rarely was there an edge in his voice. He didn't smile often, but when he did it was a warm, welcoming smile that brightened a pleasant, handsome face that was crowned by a blond crew cut. As time went on and the criticism piled up along with the incessant, inane questioning, Maris became less approachable, more difficult to interview, and less quotable.

The M&M Boys were going to be difficult, I concluded, for someone new to the beat. I found Whitey Ford, Yogi Berra, Moose Skowron, Luis Arroyo, and Tony Kubek much more helpful and accessible, and I eagerly and gratefully accepted their support, counsel, assistance, and good fellowship. But dealing with Mantle and Maris was a necessary evil for anyone covering the 1961 Yankees. Fortunately, I had formed an easy friendship with Jim Ogle of the *Newark Star-Ledger,* one of the older members of the writers' crew. I soon realized that Ogle had a special relationship with Maris and that the more I was in Ogle's company, the more available Maris was to me. I also quickly discovered that one way to engage Maris in pleasant conversation was to ask about his family. A few weeks after I arrived on the beat, Pat Maris had given birth to the couple's fourth child

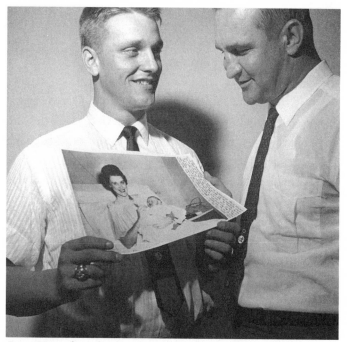

Roger Maris shows his friend, teammate, and roommate Bob Cerv a photo of his fourth child, a son, born in Kansas City on August 21, 1961. (AP IMAGES)

and Roger would soften perceptively when asked about the latest arrival to his family or, for that matter, about any of his children.

As time went on and the home run chase got hotter, I began to notice how the stress affected Maris. He seemed tormented by the pressure of the chase, uncomfortable with the unwanted attention it brought him. He would sit at his locker, or at the large, old oak table in the middle of the clubhouse, drinking coffee from a paper cup, chain-smoking unfiltered Camel cigarettes, and jiggling his legs nervously. It was soon apparent that Maris was ill at ease with the attention he was receiving. Often, he would implore the gathered media to "Write about Ellie [Howard]; he's having a great year." Or "Write about the double play Tony [shortstop Kubek] and Bobby [second baseman Richardson] turned."

Occasionally he answered questions curtly. It was not out of malice or lack of cooperation. In retrospect, I believe it was simply Maris being Maris. He got no enjoyment out of being the center of attention. He didn't play for records of for personal glory. His priorities were family, country, team. He was among the most humble of stars. When he hit a home run, there were no high fives, low fives, or chest-thumping; there was no standing at home plate to watch the flight of the ball, no curtain calls, no displays of bravado of any kind. To do any of those things would be disrespectful to the opposition and to the game; it would be demeaning the pitcher. When he hit a home run, Maris simply dropped his bat, bowed his head, trotted around the bases, and, upon reaching home plate, he surreptitiously, almost embarrassingly, accepted the hand of a teammate.

Stories popped up—usually from writers outside of New York or those who rarely visited Yankee Stadium and almost never traveled with the team—that there was envy between Maris and Mantle, a charge that flew in the face of the fact that Maris and Mantle were sharing an apartment in Queens with another Yankee, Bob Cerv and the two sluggers were the best of friends and had the utmost respect for each other.

When he learned that Maris had cancer in the early 1980s, Mantle stayed in constant touch with his old home run partner. And when Maris died, Mantle flew to Fargo for the funeral, served as a pall bearer, and was visibly distraught over the loss of a friend. These were hardly the emotions of someone who supposedly resented, failed to get along with, or envied a teammate.

"Nothing could be further from the truth," Mantle would say after he retired. "Roger and I were very close. Roger, Bob Cerv, and I shared an apartment in Queens in 1961, all during all that jealousy talk. I always liked Roger and respected him as an all-around ballplayer, not just a home run hitter. He could hit, he could run, he could field, and he could throw. He was one of the smartest players I've ever seen. He had great instincts for the game. I never saw him throw to the wrong base or miss the cutoff man, and I never saw him thrown out taking an extra base."

Maris and Mantle were rivals for the same prize, and each one wanted to be the one to grab that prize. But they were friendly rivals who pulled for one another with an attitude, albeit unspoken, "If I can't do it, I hope you do."

There were statements made, many of them handed down to this day and repeated, that Maris was misunderstood, mistreated, and portrayed unfairly by "the press"—an amorphous, nondescript group that has been painted all with the same brush, as if we were of one mind acting in concert.

Not so. We were an independent group of individuals, a cadre of a dozen or so traveling regulars later augmented by anywhere from 10 to 20 additional members as the home run race escalated, each of us with our own likes and dislikes, our own perceptions, our own relationships among the players, and, in some cases, our own agendas.

In 2001, the comedian, actor, and lifelong Yankees fan, Billy Crystal, produced and directed a television movie titled *61** that chronicles the home run chase of Maris and Mantle. The movie is entertaining, the actors portraying the principals (Thomas Jane as Mantle, Barry Pepper as Maris) are superb and thoroughly believable, and the film, for the most part, is accurate—with one glaring exception. In it, several of the writers covering the Yankees are depicted as being anti-Maris, hoping—and openly rooting—for him to fail in his bid to break Ruth's record.

Similar perceptions about the relationship between Maris and the writers covering the Yankees have been made through the years by people writing about 1961, most of whom were not there and many who had not even been born.

I *was* there and I witnessed none of this. Yes, there were times when Maris could be difficult and exasperating. (We didn't know at the time that he was receiving death threats and a steady stream of hate mail.) His remarks and actions were, at times, baffling. He was bland, uninteresting, and hardly quotable but rarely uncooperative and never hostile.

Undoubtedly, there were those writers, generally the older ones who went back to Ruth's day, who harbored thoughts that they wished Ruth's record would never be broken and others who believed that if the record were to be broken, Mantle should be the one to break it. I saw and heard none of this. I witnessed no overt rooting for Mantle, and/or against Maris, in the press box or in private conversation with the writers.

As writers covering the team, it was up to us to maintain our objectivity. We could not—or should not—root for the team to win or for certain individuals to succeed. Our interest was selling newspapers. On the other hand, as fans of the game, we were naturally excited and impressed by extraordinary performances.

Logic suggests that any writer covering the Yankees would want to see somebody, anybody, break Ruth's record. It would sell newspapers. Why wouldn't a writer want to cover something so monumental? Why wouldn't he want to be a witness to, and chronicler of, baseball history?

If there was overt rooting against Maris, it came from players who had been contemporaries of Ruth—Ty Cobb, whose career batting average of .366 is the highest in history, for one, who said, "The only thing Maris could do like Ruth is run," and Rogers Hornsby, whose .424 average in 1924 is the second-highest since 1900 to Nap Lajoie's .426 in 1901, who said Maris "couldn't carry Ruth's jock"—and from fans, many in New York, who booed him unmercifully.

*

The booing of Maris amused Mantle—"Hey, Rog, thanks for taking my fans away," he would good-naturedly chide his friend, reminded of his early days with the Yankees when he also heard boos at Yankee Stadium. He had arrived in 1951 hailed as the next Babe Ruth, Lou Gehrig, and Joe DiMaggio rolled in one and been ordained as heir apparent to DiMaggio's role as center fielder, chief run producer, and resident superstar.

Mantle was sent back to Kansas City because he was striking out too often. He was so distraught, Mantle later admitted, that he contemplated quitting baseball. He telephoned his father in Oklahoma and said, "Dad, I want you to come and get me. I can't play."

"Where you at?" asked Mutt Mantle.

"The LaSalle Hotel in Kansas City."

"I'm on my way."

The elder Mantle got in his car and made the trip from Oklahoma to Kansas City nonstop.

"When he got to the hotel," said Mantle, "the first thing he did was grab my suitcase and start throwing my clothes in it. He hadn't said a word.

"'What are you doing?' I said.

"'I'm taking you home. You can work in the mines with me. I thought I raised a man. You're nothing but a coward. If you're going to give up on yourself, you might as well come home with me instead of wasting everybody's time.'

"I had expected him to pat me on the back and say, 'Come on, Mick, hang in there. You can do it.' But he was packing to take me home. Now I was begging him to let me stay. We sat up that night and we talked quite a bit, and the next morning he went back to Oklahoma and I stayed."

Things improved for Mantle, but not right away. He returned to New York, still struggled with strikeouts, but gradually began to produce. He led the American League in strikeouts in 1952 and 1954, and the fans were still letting him have it. The booing subsided, but it didn't stop, prompting his staunchest supporter, Casey Stengel, to comment, "I never saw a man booed so much before he went to work."

It's an interesting phenomenon, a subject for a psychologist, this penchant for booing an athlete who plays for your favorite team. They booed Mantle because he wasn't Joe DiMaggio. They booed him because he wasn't living up to his promise. They booed him because he wasn't doing what they expected him to do. And they booed him mainly because they wanted him to succeed and they thought the booing would goad him into a better performance. It reminded me of a college professor of mine who often said, "I beat you because I love you." Yankees fans booed Mantle because they loved him and wanted him to attain the heights predicted for him.

It finally changed for Mantle in 1956 when he won the Triple Crown with a .353 average, 52 homers, and 130 RBIs. He had won over the fans. He was their idol, their darling, and in 1961, Mantle was their hero and Maris their villain.

Mantle was beloved by his teammates. When Ralph Houk took over as manager of the Yankees, one of his first acts was to announce that Mantle would be the team's leader, a role Mickey didn't want (he already was leading the team by example, and he never was much for titles or speech-making) but accepted nonetheless. Houk would have named Mantle team captain, but the Yankees hadn't had a captain since Lou Gehrig. When Gehrig died in 1941, the Yankees announced that the team would never have another captain, a directive that George Steinbrenner overruled when he made Thurman Munson captain in 1976.

Despite his superstar status as one of the game's greatest players, to his teammates Mantle always came across as "one of the guys." It was said that his clubhouse demeanor traced to his days as a rookie when Joe DiMaggio was coming to the end of his career but was still the team's big star. DiMaggio was described as being "aloof" and "standoffish" with most of his teammates. Mantle witnessed this behavior and supposedly vowed that if ever he was in the position of team leader like DiMaggio, he would be more outgoing and cordial to his younger teammates.

Bobby Richardson enjoyed a close relationship with both Mantle and Maris, even though he had little in common with either of them except that they were teammates with the same goals and the same competitive desire to win. Mantle's lifestyle was the complete opposite of Richardson's, and Maris was very much a loner. Yet the moral and deeply religious Richardson earned the respect and admiration of both of the M&M Boys that endured long after their playing days had ended.

"I didn't hang out with either of them when we played together, but we couldn't have had a closer relationship, especially after we retired," said Richardson. "Mantle and I had a place together in Boone, North Carolina, at Grandfather Mountain. Now there's an odd couple for you.

"Mantle was so recognizable. Everybody knew him everywhere. He came to South Carolina a year after he retired, at my invitation, and did a batting exhibition in my hometown, and the fans just mobbed him. Before the exhibition, we had a banquet. Mickey spoke and we showed a highlight film of his career that was just fantastic. It was put together by Lew Fonseca, who at the time was producing all the World Series films. At the batting exhibition, the grandstand nearly fell in there were so many people there. We gave away 2,000 Mickey Mantle bats. Tony Kubek came in just to pitch to Mickey, and Tony, kind of messing around, threw him a change-up, and Mickey swung and his leg went out from under him.

"Try as he might, Mickey couldn't hit one out of the park. Then we had an old timers' game. Mickey didn't play in it because of his leg, but Tony did and he hit one over the light stanchion in right field and that saved the day.

"We had such a big crowd we had to put a fence around the outfield to separate the people standing in the outfield from the playing field. I hit a fly ball to left field, and the left fielder went back but couldn't get to the ball because of the fence. So I circled the bases, and when I reached home plate there was Mickey and Tony both lying on the ground as if they had fainted because I hit a home run.

"Another time, Mickey came to the University of South Carolina when I was coaching their baseball team and shot an instructional film that was shown on local television for the next 10 years.

"My sons loved Mickey, and he was great with them. He had a golf tournament in Greensboro, Georgia, and I would go to play in the tournament and I'd take my boys with me. They have never forgotten how kind Mickey was to them. He would ride around in a golf cart and he would say to my boys, 'Hey, you two guys come with me. You ride in my golf cart. You can see your dad any time. I want you with me.'

"I had a great relationship with Roger as well," Richardson said. "I was very close with him. He came to South Carolina two or three times and spent the night with me. One time he came with me to watch my two boys play American Legion baseball. We had dinner in a restaurant in a little town about 10 to 15 miles from Sumter [Richardson's home] and then went to the game. There were about 2,000 people in the park and not one person recognized him, and this was only a few years after he retired. Actually, one person, a friend of mine, came up to us when the game was over and we were walking out and said to Roger, 'Boy you look a lot like Roger Maris.'

"When I retired from baseball, the Yankees gave me a wonderful gun cabinet made out of solid oak inscribed by all the players. On his own, Roger gave me a beautiful wristwatch with my uniform No. 1 inscribed on it."

*

On August 4, 1961, Hawaii's second year of statehood, future president Barack Obama was born in Kapi'olani Maternity and Gynecological Hospital in Honolulu. On that day, some 5,000 miles and five time zones away in the Bronx and two days after Mantle tied Maris at 40 homers, Maris ended an eight-game homerless drought and reclaimed the lead with his 41st home run, a three-run shot in the first inning off Camilo Pascual of the Twins. But two days later, also against the Twins, Mantle went on a three-home run barrage in a doubleheader and jumped back ahead of Maris (most observers believed to stay), 43–41.

Mantle had been late getting to Yankee Stadium that day because his wife Merlyn was arriving by train from Dallas (she disliked flying) and Mickey went to Penn Station to meet her.

"First game she's seen all year," said Mantle, who homered in the first and third innings of the 15-inning first game and in the second inning of the second game. He would play all 24 innings of the Yankees' sweep, a total of 6:42 of baseball, and when it ended, he was two home runs up on Maris and 18 games ahead of Ruth's record pace.

"I'd rather not talk about it," said Mantle, when reporters asked him to assess his prospects at breaking the record. "I hear too much of that stuff."

Mantle did reveal that since spring training he had been using a bat borrowed from catcher John Blanchard that weighed 33 ounces and was 35 inches long, a half inch longer than the bat he used in the 1960 season.

Like Mantle, Maris also swung a 35-inch, 33-ounce bat, the difference being that Maris' bat had a thicker handle. When he first came to the Yankees in 1951, Mantle used a 36-ounce bat. Gradually through the years, Mantle switched to lighter bats with thinner handles in keeping with the times, the theory being that bat speed, not weight, was conducive to hitting a baseball great distances.

The downside to the thin-handle bats is that they break more easily. In 1950, the Yankees' bill for bats, at a cost of $3 per, was $1,546. Ten years later, the bill had jumped to $2,250. In the 1950s and 1960s, virtually all major league bats were supplied by two companies, Hillerich & Bradsby of Louisville, Kentucky, and Adirondack Bats, Inc., of Dolgeville, New York, and both had contracts with every major league club.

As time went on, new companies entered the bat-making business so that today teams no longer furnish bats to their players. Players are responsible for acquiring their own bats. However, many star players have contracts with bat companies who supply them with product. Many of those players who do not have bat contracts are equipped with bats by various companies just for using them.

In his heyday, Babe Ruth's bat weighed a mighty 42 ounces and, according to Frank Ryan, a spokesman for Hillerich & Bradsby, the Babe was contemplating using an ever heavier bat.

In an article in the *New York Times* of August 20, 1961, Ryan said, "We have an old order on file from the Yankees for 52-ounce bats for Ruth. Frankly, I doubt if the Babe ever used them. Our records show he favored a 42-ounce bat in his prime and never used one that weighed less than 38 ounces.

"Many other players of that era also preferred heavy bats. Ty Cobb swung a real piece of lumber—it was only 34½ inches long but weighed 42 ounces. Of our regular models, the heaviest I know of was Edd Roush's 48-ouncer."

On August 7, the Angels arrived in the Bronx for the start of a four-game series. In the first game, the Angels led 1–0 in the bottom of the third when, with one out, Bobby Richardson doubled and moved to third on Clete Boyer's ground-out to shortstop. Maris came to bat with a runner on third and two out and the bizarre happened. Roger Maris bunted!

A guy with 41 home runs, with a chance to break the most prestigious record in sports, gave away a precious at-bat by bunting! He spotted third baseman Eddie Yost playing back behind the bag, and he dropped a perfect bunt that rolled down the third-base line and came to rest just in front of third base. Richardson scored from third and the game was tied 1–1. The Yankees would go on to win 4–1 for their fifth straight victory (they would increase their winning streak to nine and open a four-game lead on the Tigers in the American League). Maris' bunt paid off. The end justified the means. Or did it?

"I told you this game wasn't all made up of home runs," Maris said to a group of reporters at his locker after the game. "Bunts count, too. If they're going to play back on me, I'm going to bunt. Every time I have a man on third, I'll think about bunting. You put a man on third and I don't care if I have the hottest bat in the league. My job is to try to score him. I've thought about it a lot, but I never got the right pitch to do it. With Boyer up, I noticed Yost laying back, and that's when I decided to bunt if I got the right pitch.

"If we can go on to win the pennant, I'll be satisfied if I don't hit another homer. I'll take my 41. Sure, I like to hit homers, but I'm not swinging for them. Even if we had already won the pennant and I see a chance to win a game with a bunt, I'll do it."

"I guess that shows he's not very greedy," said manager Ralph Houk. "He must not have been thinking of the record. He must have been thinking of winning, which speaks well for him. It's good for the club and it's good for the manager."

Whitey Ford said seeing a big home run hitter lay down a bunt to help the team when he's chasing a record, "makes a pitcher know he's out there trying to win and not thinking of himself."

Ryne Duren, who had been traded to the Angels by the Yankees earlier that year said, "I can't say I was surprised.

He's going for the pennant first. That's the kind of player he is."

The bunt caught the attention of everybody in baseball. Judging from their remarks, it also earned him the respect of his teammates. But what did they really think? There were some who saw the bunt as a sign Maris was throwing in the towel on trying to catch Ruth and conceding the home run race to Mantle.

Chapter Twelve

Streaking

Just when so many baseball experts were writing off his chances of challenging Babe Ruth's single-season record, Roger Maris went on another of his frequent and typical home run streaks to insinuate himself back into the race against Ruth.

On August 11, Maris and Mickey Mantle both hit home runs against the Senators in Washington. Maris connected in the fifth inning for his 42nd, ending a seven-game homerless drought. Mantle connected in the seventh inning for No. 44. After the game—as was their wont or their instructions from their sports editors—reporters crowded around Maris' locker.

"Write about someone else," Maris begged. "[Tony] Kubek for instance. He's been doing a great job all year, and he never gets his name in the paper."

But Maris could not be ignored. He hit a home run in each of the four games in Washington and drew even with Mantle at 45. The focus—and the pressure—shifted back to Maris, and for the first time he began to show the effects of that pressure.

"Don't ask me about that blankety-blank record," he growled. "I don't want to talk about it. All I'm interested in is winning the pennant."

On the bus from Griffith Stadium to the airport, I found myself seated next to Maris, who was in one of his rare gregarious moods, partly because of his home run splurge against the Senators, but most likely because in less than two weeks, the Yankees would play three games in Kansas City and he would see his wife and children for the first time in almost a month. Without prompting, he began what seemed a stream of consciousness litany of his hopes, his joys, and his regrets.

"I read an article by an old timer [a former player] the other day that really teed me off," he said. "He said they [hitters] had it tougher in his day because the infielders were better and the runners were faster. That's a lot of bull. Doesn't he realize that the gloves now are much better?

"Then you hear a lot about what short porches we have to shoot at. They had short porches in the old days, too. Some were shorter than we have now. Take Fenway Park! That used to be shorter until they moved the fence back in right field. And Cleveland, when they played in League Park, was shorter than Municipal Stadium.

"I don't care if a fence is 200', you still have to reach it, and if you do, you deserve a home run.

"One guy wrote a letter to *The Sporting News* saying he'd hate to see a bum like me break Ruth's record. What am I supposed to do? I admire Ruth. He was the greatest. But they make it sound like I'd be doing something sacrilegious if I broke his record.

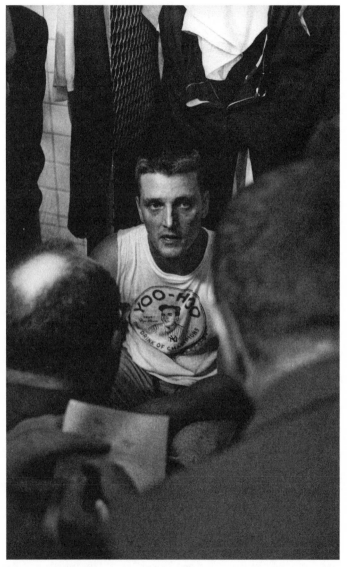

Regrettably, baseball had not yet adopted the practice of conducting postgame interviews in private rooms. (PHOTO BY C&G COLLECTIONS/GETTY IMAGES)

"This doesn't pertain to me, but it does to Mick," he continued. "The Commissioner says he won't recognize the record if it comes after 154 games. That's not fair to Mickey. If you check, you'll see that Mantle won't come to bat as often as Ruth did because of walks. Why doesn't he figure the record on times at bat instead of games to be fair with Mick? With me, it's different. I'll come to bat more than Ruth."

Emboldened by his candor, I ventured a question. I asked Maris if he could explain why he goes into home run droughts, why he might go 30, 40 times at bat without hitting one out and then hit four home runs in four games.

"I wish I knew," he replied. "I'm getting my pitch, but I was getting my pitch in New York, too. I hit a lot of good balls on the ground. If I get my pitch and hit it the way I want to hit it, it's a home run. Sometimes you get your pitch and you don't hit it right. The difference between a home run and a line drive is what, an eighth of an inch?"

*

Maris' home run on August 11 not only ended a seven-game homerless drought, but it also touched off a streak of seven home runs in six games that enabled him to reclaim the league lead from Mantle, 48–45, and surge 17 games ahead of Ruth's record pace.

On August 16, the 13th anniversary of Babe Ruth's death, the Yankees met the White Sox in an afternoon game at Yankee Stadium. A crowd of 29,728, including 7,621 Yankee Juniors and Babe Ruth Leaguers, received souvenir booklets containing a tribute to Ruth and enumerating his baseball records. On hand was Mrs. Babe Ruth, who posed for photographs with Maris and Mantle before the game. As if to honor Ruth—or issue a challenge against him—Maris hit two home runs, his 47th and 48th, and then had to talk about the man whose record he was approaching.

He has nothing against Ruth, Maris said. "Without him, where would we all be?" His complaint is with those who question his right to be chasing the great man's record and with the thought that he is tampering with the Ruth legend. He's tired and he's unappreciated (the boos, remember) and he misses his family.

"People think it's fun playing ball every day," he said. "To me, it's just a way to make money. You know that guy on television, *The Millionaire*? Well, if he came to me tomorrow with a check for a million, I'd be on my way home right away."

Lost in the excitement and anticipation of the home run race was the cold, hard fact of life as a baseball player. Often it was drudgery, a daily grind that in 1961 began for a player when he reported for spring training in the middle of February and ended, if he was lucky enough to play on a team that made it to the World Series, in the middle of October. It was eight solid, continuous, uninterrupted months of pressure—and questions for Mickey Mantle and Roger Maris—with hardly any relief.

On the Yankees' 1961 schedule were 14 doubleheaders, 11 of them on Sunday plus the Fourth of July, Labor Day, and August 2. Of their 162 games, only 70 were scheduled as night games. There were 26 off-days, most of them Mondays and Thursdays, which were usually used for travel. Because the writers covering the Yankees traveled with the team in

1961, they were working on the players' days off. That meant that even on their days off, there were questions asked of the players and no escape for them. The writers were thrown in with the players on the plane, on the bus going from the airport to the hotel and from the hotel to the airport, in the hotel lobby, in the hotel coffee shop, at the ballpark if there was a practice, and in the clubhouse before and after games. And always there were questions, questions, questions, most of them directed at Mantle and Maris.

Baseball, unlike every other sport, is an everyday game. Whereas Muhammad Ali might fight two or three times a year, Joe Namath would play once a week, Michael Jordan would play two or three times a week, and Tiger Woods plays only on weekends, in 1961 Mantle and Maris were under the microscope, in the crosshairs, under surveillance, and subject to cross-examination every day.

Maris' home run streak ended on August 17. He batted four times, struck out once, and grounded out three times against the White Sox, who won the battle but lost the war (the Yankees won for the 14th time in 18 games). Determined to shut down Maris, White Sox manager Al Lopez played three men on the right side of the infield, and Maris hit three ground balls. But it wasn't the shift that beat him, Maris said.

"Let 'em shift," he said. "If I hit the ball right, they're not going to get it anyway."

Fatigue (pressure?) appeared to be gripping both Mantle and Maris as the Yankees opened a grueling 13-game road trip with a 5–1 defeat in Cleveland. Between them, Mantle and Maris were hitless in eight at-bats with four strikeouts against Jim (Mudcat) Grant.

What made the pitiful performance of the M&M Boys so disheartening is that the Indians, who had been averaging 5,000 fans per game in recent weeks, drew 37,840 for the opener of the series against the Yankees, most of them there to see Mantle and/or Maris hit a home run. That was obvious from the pregame announcement of the starting lineups. The names of Maris and Mantle were greeted with rousing cheers while the names of the home-team starters were greeted mostly with jeers.

With his 0-for-4, Mantle had just two hits and no home runs in his last 17 at-bats. His legs ached, but he wouldn't ask manager Houk for a day off because there was a pennant to be won.

Like Mantle, Maris also was 0-for-4 with two strikeouts against Grant. For the second straight game, he failed to get the ball out of the infield. He was hitless in eight at-bats, homerless in 10. And he was fatigued.

"I'm tired all the time," Maris said. "The bat gets heavier this time of year. I can't wait for the season to end."

In Las Vegas, odds-maker Jimmy (The Greek) Snyder was offering 5-to-6 "do or die" on either Mantle or Maris to break Ruth's record. That meant you pick either one of the two to break the record and put up $6 to win $5. The Greek also was offering 12-to-5 that Maris and Mantle would not both hit 61 home runs within the 154-game schedule.

Mantle's slump had reached 3-for-21 when, on August 20 in Cleveland, he belted his 46th home run off Jim Perry in the first inning. In the same game, Maris snapped his hitless streak at 13 at-bats and his homerless streak at 15 at-bats with home run No. 49 in the third inning, also off Perry.

Two days later in Los Angeles, in the first game of a three-game series against the Angels, Maris belted his 50th home run against Ken McBride. It was the 14th time in baseball history that 50 home runs in a season had been reached, putting Maris in elite company. Eight different players had done it—Babe Ruth four times, Jimmie Foxx and Ralph Kiner twice, Hank Greenberg, Hack Wilson, Johnny Mize, Willie Mays, and Mickey Mantle once each—all of them eventually enshrined in the Baseball Hall of Fame.

*

On the day after his 50th home run, Mantle and Maris became movie stars. They, along with Yogi Berra, fulfilled a commitment to film a scene in the movie *That Touch of Mink* starring Doris Day and Cary Grant. Born Archibald Alexander Leach in Horfield, Bristol, England, in 1904, Grant did not come to the United States until 1920 at the age of 16. Nonetheless he became an avid baseball fan who, in his later years, spent many days and nights at Yankee Stadium watching the Yankees as the guest of owner George Steinbrenner.

In the movie, Grant plays a wealthy playboy who meets Day, a poor girl from Upper Sandusky, Ohio. In an effort to impress her, Grant uses his considerable influence to arrange for the two of them to be in the Yankees dugout (reproduced on the Hollywood set) during a game where they interact with the three players, each of whom has one speaking line. In the scene, Day disagrees with a call by the umpire against a Yankee batter.

The M&M Boys, Roger Maris (left) and Mickey Mantle, had cameo roles in a 1961 movie, That Touch of Mink. *Here the Yankees receive an autographed baseball from the film's star, Doris Day.* (AP IMAGES)

"Hey, ump," she shouts. "Shake your head. Your eyeballs are stuck."

When the umpire, played by former American League arbiter Art Passarella, berates her for yelling at him, Day turns to Maris, Mantle, and Berra for support.

Covering the event in the *New York Times,* Murray Schumach wrote, "A virtual revolution occurred on a movie set here today when flocks of men, women, and children ignored both Cary Grant and Doris Day to plead for the signatures of three men who had never acted before this morning.

"The actors making their debuts were Mickey Mantle, Roger Maris, and Yogi Berra…. Attired in their New York Yankee uniforms, the three baseball stars completely outshone Mr. Grant and Miss Day as far as outsiders were concerned.

"Blasé movie crews, who have been spending many years watching all sorts of movie idols with relative indifference, could not wait to cluster around the ballplayers before shooting, after shooting, and during breaks in the filming…. The ban against nonworking children on a movie set was lifted for this occasion.

"When the baseball players had ended their hour and a half of movie work, Berra grinned, shrugged, and remarked, 'This is like stealing money, ain't it?'

"Delbert Mann, the director, was delighted with the efficiency of the athletes in the acting role. He was particularly impressed with the performance of Berra, whose acting was very full, with an improvised shrug, shake of the head, and a hurt look under raised eyebrows.

"'I didn't suggest any of those things to Berra,' said Mr. Mann. 'He is just an outgoing type.'

"Mr. Passarella, who had umpired many games behind the plate when Berra was catching, snorted at this understatement.

"'Yogi,' he said, 'made my life miserable. He never stopped talking while I was working.'

"Maris, perhaps because he is now within ten home runs of Babe Ruth's 1927 record of 60, seemed the most tense. Mantle, who has 46 homers, was slightly more relaxed.

"At noon, when shooting with the ballplayers ended, they were besieged by the autograph seekers, many of whom had come prepared with baseballs, baseball gloves, baseball programs, as well as notebooks and pieces of paper. Among those humbly seeking autographs was Robert Arthur, executive producer of the movie, who had received a telephoned request from his nephew in New York."

✳

Interest in the home run race in general, and in Maris and Mantle in particular, had reached a fever pitch and was having a profound impact on the nation's television viewing habits. In an article in the *New York Times* on August 21, John P. Shanley wrote, "A couple of producers named Maris and Mantle are giving television a much-needed series of injections of excitement these days.

"This New York Yankee home run production team has created a fever of interest in the television screen that normally would not develop before October and World Series time.

"In office buildings, bars, and other locations, the clusters of fans around TV sets testify to the extraordinary interest in the efforts by the two Yankee sluggers to approach Babe Ruth's record of 60 home runs in a season.

"Some viewers, including former Brooklyn Dodger partisans, have begun to watch the baseball telecasts on a part-time basis. They switch to the game at about the time that they expect Roger Maris and Mickey Mantle to come to bat. Otherwise maintaining their longstanding contempt for the Yankees, they seek diversion elsewhere.

"At WPIX [Channel 11], which televises the Yankee games, it has been reported that the number of persons watching them on TV already has increased by 16 percent over last year, according to rating surveys."

*

Maris had just one more hit, a triple, in the final two games in Los Angeles before the Yankees moved on to Kansas City for a three-game weekend series. In the Friday night series opener, Ralph Terry pitched a five-hitter and improved his record to 11–1 with a 3–0 victory in front of a crowd of 30,830, the largest of the season in Kansas City's Municipal Stadium.

The second game of the series on Saturday night outdrew the first night's crowd, as 32,149 turned out to watch Bill Stafford win his 11th game with a three-hitter in a 5–1 Yankees victory.

The Yankees completed a three-game sweep on Sunday with an 8–7 victory as Whitey Ford went five innings to improve his record to 22–3.

It was also a clean sweep for the Athletics at the box office as they drew their largest crowd of the season for the third straight game with 34,065 in attendance. It made the three-game total, no doubt attributable to the excitement of the home run race, 97,044. In nine games against the Yankees at Municipal Stadium, the Athletics drew 199,966, an average of 22,218 per game. In 71 home games against all other opposition, the Athletics drew 483,851, or 6,814 per game.

To date, the Yankees (the M&M Boys?) had drawn the largest one-day attendance in eight of the nine other American League cities, the only exception being Detroit where a doubleheader between the Tigers and White Sox had so far attracted the season high at Tiger Stadium.

In 67 road games, the Yankees had played before 1,557,266 customers, an average of 23,243 per game. The average would have been higher but for the fact that they had played nine of those games in tiny Wrigley Field, the temporary home of the expansion Los Angeles Angels with its capacity of 19,800. The Yankees would finish the season with a major league–record road attendance of 1,946,679.

Maris had only one hit in 11 at-bats in the three games in Kansas City, surprising because he had always hit well when he returned home. But his one hit was home run No. 51 in the middle game of the three-game series, and the Yankees' 129th game, on August 26.

The Yankees would close out the month of August with three games in Minnesota on the 29th, 30th, and 31st—with Maris a comfortable five home runs ahead of his teammate Mantle, 51–46.

Joe Altobelli had started the 1961 season as the property of the Minnesota Twins, playing for the Syracuse Chiefs in the AAA International League. Syracuse is only about 250 miles from Yankee Stadium, but in perception the distance is light years, and Altobelli, consumed with his own effort to get back to the major leagues, was pretty much oblivious to what was going on in the Bronx where his former teammate,

Roger Maris, was not only the talk of the borough, but of the entire city, the state, and the nation.

Altobelli's mission was achieved on July 1 when he was summoned to Minnesota by the Twins' new manager, Sam Mele, who had replaced Cookie Lavagetto two weeks earlier.

"The Twins' ballpark had a large message board and if we weren't playing the Yankees and Roger or Mickey hit a home run, they would put it up on the board," said Altobelli. "That was how I was able to follow the home run race.

"When the Yankees came to Minnesota, I tried to get in touch with Maris to get together with him. I called his hotel, but there was no answer. When I saw him at the ballpark, he apologized and said he wasn't picking up his phone and he couldn't even leave the hotel because fans, hundreds of them, would be hanging around the lobby waiting for him, hoping to get his autograph."

Maris would not hit another home run in the month of August, but he would pick up another endorsement, this one from Casey…no, not Stengel. This "Casey" was an IBM 1401 computer housed at the Statistical Tabulating Corporation's New York Branch. Casey predicted that Maris would, but Mantle wouldn't, break Babe Ruth's home run record. Casey the computer estimated there were 55 chances out of 100 that Maris would do it and even predicted that Maris would hit home run No. 61 in the Yankees 154th game. On the other hand, Mantle's chances of hitting 61 home runs within the 154-game schedule, Casey estimated, were just two out of 100.

Despite hitting only one home run in the last nine days of August, Maris still would go into the dreaded month of September in good shape to take aim at Ruth's record.

He would not have to worry about falling victim to Ruth's torrid pace of 17 home runs in September. Entering the final month of the season, he was only nine home runs away from Ruth's record and six games ahead of the Babe's record pace.

Mantle closed August with a flourish. He hit his 47th homer on August 30. On August 31, he hit No. 48, one of three home runs by the Yankees, who set an American League record with 195 home runs and were taking dead aim on the major league record of 221 shared by the 1947 New York Giants and 1956 Cincinnati Reds. Heading into September, Mantle was one game ahead of Ruth's pace and poised for a finishing kick.

Chapter Thirteen

Big Game Hunting

"What does it profit a man to gain the whole world but forfeit his soul?" —Mark 8:36

AND WHAT DOES IT PROFIT ROGER MARIS, if he was to remain true to his word, to break the home run record but lose the pennant? Now, as September arrived, the home run record chase had been put on the back burner. The focus shifted to the pennant race with the ever-menacing, tenacious, refuse-to-cave-in Detroit Tigers arriving at Yankee Stadium for a critical three-game series on September 1, 2, and 3, in second place, a game and a half behind the Yankees.

Buffeted by the power of Norm Cash, leading the American League in batting; Rocky Colavito; and the all-around brilliance of Al Kaline, the Tigers had managed to withstand the two-pronged home run assault of the Yankees' M&M Boys (Colavito and Cash, Detroit's C&C Boys, had combined for 71 homers) and remain within striking distance of first place. Now they were in a position to vault over the Yankees into the league lead. It would take an unlikely sweep of the three games in the Yankees' home stadium in front of what figured to be three wild and raucous crowds. The Tigers were confident because lined up, rested, and ready to face the Yankees were their three best pitchers, Don Mossi, 14–3; Frank Lary, 19–7; and Jim Bunning, 15–10.

In his career, Maris faced Bunning 91 times, more than any other pitcher except Camilo Pascual (125 plate appearances), Bill Monbouquette (105 PAs), Frank Lary (101 PAs), and Milt Pappas (95 PAs). Maris had three doubles off Bunning, two triples, five home runs, and 11 RBIs. He was walked 16 times, struck out nine times, had a .324 batting average, a .451 on-base percentage, and a .622 slugging average.

"There's a list of every home run Roger Maris hit in 1961 with the date, the number of the home run, and the name of the pitcher that threw it," said Bunning, the only man to be a member of both the Baseball Hall of Fame and the United States Senate. "I'm not on that list. I was so proud that I didn't make that list, but I almost did. We played a series in Tiger Stadium in late September. I thought Roger had hit a home run off me. He hit a ball below the fence that hit one of the iron girders and ricocheted almost to second base. He got a triple. He missed a home run by inches.

"I am on the list of Mantle's career home runs. I gave up his 200th [July 26, 1957, in Yankee Stadium]. I didn't want to be on that list, either, but now they have card shows for pitchers that threw Mantle's 100th, 200th, 300th, 400th, and 500th home runs." (In 2002, a baseball signed by both Roger Maris and Tracy Stallard, the pitcher who served up Maris' 61st home run, sold at auction for $351,000.)

"I followed the home run race in 1961 closely. I rooted for Mantle and Maris to break the record. I wanted a modern guy that I played against to hold the record. Of course, I wanted to beat them and I didn't want to be on their list, but I wanted them to break the record. All the pitchers that played against them didn't want to be on their list, but they liked it when one of them hit one.

"I thought Mantle was going to do it, until he got hurt. I broadcast the World Series in Cincinnati with Waite Hoyt and you could see that Mantle was still not healthy.

"Strangely, I had better luck getting Mantle out than I did Maris [in 69 plate appearances, Mantle had 12 hits off Bunning, one double, and six home runs, 23 strikeouts and a .207 average]. After [Mantle] hit a ball over the roof in Tiger Stadium off me, I never threw him another off-speed pitch. Never! That's the only pitch he ever hit off me. Finally, I wised up enough to throw him nothing but hard stuff in. Roger was like pitching to Ted Williams. If you kept the ball down, you had a reasonable chance of keeping it in the ballpark.

"My relationship with Maris was always positive. He was a very quiet guy, kind of reclusive. He just wanted to be with his wife and family. A lot of us were like that. When you get thrown into the big leagues, if you're shy—and some of us are and were—the exposure to major league writers and broadcasters and the things that you do, it's your private life, and you want to keep it that way.

"I knew what Roger was doing that year. He was trying to hide, and it's impossible to hide when you're doing what he was doing. He had all kinds of emotional problems dealing with that much publicity because he was a Fargo guy. But he was the same way as long as I knew him, from the minor leagues on up. If he didn't hit and do things with the bat— by the way, he was probably the best all-around outfielder at that time, everything—throwing, running bases, everything. He was that good. He was the quietest superstar I have ever seen. I had deep respect for Roger Maris."

A crowd of 65,566, the Yankees' largest single-night game attendance of the year, turned out to Yankee Stadium on a steamy Friday night for the opener of a critical three-game series between the first-place Yankees and the second-place Tigers.

Earlier in the day, the Baltimore Orioles announced that Paul Richards, a native of Waxahachie, Texas, had resigned as their manager to become the general manager of the expansion Houston team that would begin play in 1962. The Houston team, to be called the Houston Colt .45s, and an expansion team in New York, to be called the Mets, would join the National League and raise the number of teams in that league from eight to 10, just like in the American League.

To replace Richards as manager, the Orioles chose one of Richards' coaches, Luman Harris. The change in Baltimore's manager would come into play in the final days of Maris' pursuit of the single-season home run record.

For now, however, the focus in baseball was not on Harris or Richards, the Baltimore Orioles, or even the home run race. It was on the start of a three-game American League showdown series in the Bronx between the first-place New York Yankees and the second-place Detroit Tigers. When the game got underway, the partisan Yankees crowd sat squirming with anxiety and anticipation as Whitey Ford matched zeroes with the Tigers' Don Mossi, like Ford a left-hander. Mossi was a crafty, 32-year-old, eight-year major league veteran with large ears who has been described as "looking like a taxi cab with its doors open." He had been an excellent relief pitcher for the Cleveland Indians, but he was traded to Detroit in 1959 and turned into a starter.

Both pitchers allowed one hit in the first inning, a two-out triple by Kaline off of Ford and a one-out single by Tony Kubek off of Mossi. But Ford held Kaline at third by retiring Colavito on a ground ball to shortstop, and Mossi followed Kubek's hit by striking out Maris and Mantle.

With two outs and a runner on first in the top of the fifth inning, manager Ralph Houk trotted out to the pitcher's mound accompanied by team trainer Gus Mauch. After a few minutes of discussion, Houk and Mauch left the mound and with them was Ford, the Yankees' ace pitcher and 22-game winner, bringing a shudder of fear to the large stadium crowd. It was later revealed that Ford had strained a hip muscle in the fourth inning. He was replaced on the mound by Bud Daley, another left-hander.

Mossi was using all his guile, changing speeds masterfully as he set the Yankees down with one hit through the first four innings. From Kubek's one-out single in the first to Yogi Berra's one-out single in the fifth, he had retired 12 consecutive Yankees. And Daley had picked up where Ford left off, getting out of the fifth inning and surviving a sixth inning in which the Tigers had two singles, a walk, and a passed ball but did not score.

Tension in the big ballpark was palpable as the game moved into the seventh inning, still scoreless. Daley retired the Tigers in order in the top of the seventh. Mantle, who had struck out his first two times up, led off the bottom of the seventh and hit a weak pop-up to shortstop. He put his head down, slumped his shoulders, and returned quietly to the Yankees' dugout. Moments later, out of the dugout came flying a batting helmet that looked suspiciously like the one Mantle had worn at bat.

In the top of the eighth, Billy Bruton walked with one out, and Kaline followed with a single that chased Bruton to third. Trying to stretch his single into a double, Kaline was cut down at second by Yogi Berra, who started in left field against a left-handed pitcher for the first time all season.

"I put Yogi out there for his defense," Houk joked later. "Yogi always makes the right play."

Berra, however, wouldn't take credit for his throwing or his wisdom.

"I just threw it," he mumbled. "I didn't even know if he [Kaline] was going. I knew I couldn't get Bruton, so I just threw to second. I made up my mind before he hit it, if I get the ball I'll throw to second because the runner will probably be going to break up the double play.

"I knew the ball was going to carom off the fence, and I was lucky it caromed into my glove. I still throw like a catcher. When you catch you just get rid of the ball. In the outfield, you're supposed to take a step to get something on the throw."

He wasn't boasting. He wasn't even taking credit for saving the game. That's not Yogi's style.

"Tomorrow I'll probably get hit on the head with a fly ball," he said.

With Bruton on third, two out, first base open, and the dangerous Colavito due up, Houk went to the mound to talk to his left-hander, Daley.

"I asked him if he wanted to walk [right-handed-hitting] Colavito and pitch to [left-handed-hitting] Cash. When he didn't give me a direct answer, I said, 'Go get him out.'"

Colavito hit a screaming line drive into the left-field seats that hooked foul.

"I was scared at first," said Houk. "I thought I made the wrong decision. When the count went to 3–1, I decided to walk [Colavito]."

That brought up Cash, the league's leading hitter. Daley got him to hit a foul pop to catcher Elston Howard.

In the bottom of the eighth, the Yankees wasted a leadoff double by Clete Boyer. Luis Arroyo replaced Daley in the top of the ninth and set the Tigers down in order.

In the bottom of the ninth, Mossi got Maris to lift a fly ball to right and struck out Mantle for the third time, the second time looking. His frustration bubbling over, Mantle had words for plate umpire Joe Paparella, who showed remarkable restraint by not ejecting Mantle from so critical a game.

With the Yankees' most dangerous hitters, the feared M&M Boys, gone, extra innings seemed inevitable. But Elston Howard singled to center and Berra chased him to third with a single to right. Moose Skowron then bounced a hit past third baseman Steve Boros to deliver Howard with the winning run.

It was a crushing 1–0 defeat for the Tigers, and especially for Mossi, who had pitched so gallantly and effectively but trudged solemnly off the field with his fourth defeat instead of his 15th win.

Tigers' hopes soared when Rocky Colavito hit his 40th home run of the season, off Ralph Terry in the first inning of the second game of the series, on Saturday afternoon, September 2, the game played in oppressive and unseasonable heat as the thermometer reached 96 degrees. The home run, which followed Kaline's single, gave the Tigers a two-run lead for their ace, 19-game-winner Frank Lary, a renowned Yankee killer who had a career record of 26–9 against them.

But Terry buckled down to hold the Tigers to no runs and four hits over the next six-and-two-thirds innings. The Yankees started pecking away at Lary with a run in the second on a walk to Mantle and Skowron's RBI double, and another in the fourth on a double by Maris, a passed ball, and a successful squeeze bunt by Mantle.

With the score tied 2–2 in the sixth, Maris blasted his 52rd home run. Mantle followed by grounding to second and as he did, pulled a muscle in his left forearm. He refused to leave the game. When he came to bat in the eighth, the pain in his arm was so severe, he bunted.

According to Houk, Mantle told him he couldn't swing the bat, "but he would bunt every time up if I would let him stay in for defensive purposes in center field. He had no business playing, but I let him."

The Yankees broke the game open with four runs in the eighth, the last two on Maris' second home run of the game, and 53rd of the season, the most ever by any Yankee not named Babe Ruth, off left-hander Hank Aguirre. Luis Arroyo replaced Terry in the eighth, faced four batters, and retired them all, three on strikeouts, to nail down the 7–2 victory and collect his 26th save of the season.

Maris' two home runs enabled him to surge eight games ahead of Ruth's record pace, but Roger was more excited that the Yankees had opened a three-and-a-half game lead on the Tigers and were moving in for the three-game sweep in the series finale on Sunday afternoon.

Mantle tested his sore left arm in batting practice, hit a few balls into the seats, and proclaimed himself ready to play. Then he proved it by belting two home runs. He hit his 49th home run in the first inning after Maris singled with two outs. Yogi Berra went back-to-back with Mantle to give the Yanks a 3–1 lead.

The Yankees increased their lead to 4–1 in the fifth before the Tigers staged a gallant comeback with a run in the sixth, another in the eighth, and two in the top of the ninth to go ahead 5–4 and keep their hopes alive. But the Yankees rallied in the bottom of the ninth. Mantle's 50th home run tied it. Berra followed with a single, Arroyo sacrificed him to second, Skowron was intentionally walked, and Howard sent everybody home with a three-run homer that gave the Yankees an 8–5 victory, a sweep of the three-game series, and a four-and-a-half game lead over the Tigers. Arroyo won two of the three games and saved the third.

Mantle's two home runs enabled him to reach the 50-homer plateau for the second time in his career and put him back in the chase for Ruth's record, now two games ahead of the Babe. Between them, Mantle and Maris had 103 homers, only four away from the all-time record of 107 by two players on the same team, Ruth and Gehrig for the 1927 Yankees.

The three games had drawn 171,503 paying customers, a Yankee Stadium record for a three-game series, and the sweep left the perception that the Yankees had killed off the Tigers. They would go on to win 13 straight games and put the Tigers away, and they would soon clinch their 26th American League pennant. It meant that baseball observers could now resume focusing their attention on the chase of Babe Ruth's record for home runs in a season.

Chapter Fourteen

Boo!

ONE DAY AFTER FORCING HIS WAY BACK into the home run race, Mickey Mantle's chances of catching Babe Ruth (or Roger Maris) suffered a devastating blow when his left arm stiffened and was so sore that he couldn't swing a bat. He had to scratch himself from a doubleheader against the Senators.

"His left arm was swollen more than it was Saturday," observed manager Ralph Houk. "I don't know when he'll be ready. It will be up to him. When he tells me he can play, he'll play."

The official records will show that Mantle played in the first game of the doubleheader, but he entered the game in the ninth inning for defense and never came to bat. It was not a good time for Mantle to have to forego seven or eight at-bats against a team that he traditionally punished and with Maris in the throes of a hitless streak of 11 at-bats. Maris was 0–8 in the doubleheader and once again heard the Yankee Stadium boo birds.

Here was a player who had hit 53 home runs and still had a great chance to break the most prestigious record in baseball and he was being booed by the hometown fans. It defied reason, and it caused Maris to lash out at his tormentors.

"They're a lousy bunch of frontrunners, that's what they are," Maris stormed when asked about being booed in his home stadium. "Hit a home run and they love you, but make an out and they start booing. Give me the fans in Kansas City anytime. There's no place that can compare with the people there."

Maris said he had been hearing it all year from fans in the right-field stands, but he played center field in place of Mantle in the doubleheader and the boo birds moved with him.

"There are a few faces you see all the time," he said. "I know who they are, the same ones always giving me a hard time. That's okay as long as they leave me alone outside the ballpark. They never bother you when you're face-to-face with them."

Maris was told that fans pay their money, so they have a right to boo.

"I didn't ask them to come," he replied. "If they keep giving me a hard time, I'll do my job on the field and give them what they pay to see. But they better not come around after the game and bother me for autographs and things. I can walk through 15 million of them and never look at one of them. I've got about as much love for them as they've got for me. Those people who boo, they just don't know any better."

By his own admission, Maris was very much a loner. He was always one of the first to arrive at the ballpark and among the last to leave. When his work was done, he returned to the apartment in Queens he shared with Mantle and Bob Cerv, and once there, he wanted to be left alone.

"I guess I'm antisocial," he said. "I don't even know my next-door neighbors, and that's the way I want it. I'm not a good mixer. I just like to keep to myself."

The day after the doubleheader sweep of the Senators, Mantle arrived at Yankee Stadium and told Houk that his injured left forearm felt fine. The day off had produced a miracle.

"I felt strong as hell," Mantle said. "I felt more like playing. When you have to play every day you get tired. You feel drowsy, and sometimes you have to force yourself to go out in the field."

Houk was cautious.

"I told him to test it in batting practice. If it felt all right, I'd play him."

Mantle spent an hour in the whirlpool, took some ultrasound, and then went out to take batting practice and it felt all right. It felt better than all right.

"I felt it just a little, but I knew I wouldn't hurt it any more if I played," said Mantle, who switched from his usual 33-ounce bat to Cerv's 36-ounce bat. "I figured the heavier bat would cut down on my swing. I wanted to swing easy so I didn't hurt the arm again. That's how I hurt it in the first place, swinging too hard."

Mantle swung so easy at the first pitch he saw from Joe McClain that he sent it into the 20th row of the third deck in right field for his 51st home run, only two behind Maris. With one easy swing, Mantle had not only jumped back into the home run race, he had once again become the favorite to surpass Ruth because of his penchant for hitting home runs in bunches (five in his last six games) coupled with Maris' penchant for cold streaks (his current hitless streak had reached 15 at-bats and he had just 10 hits in his last 73 at-bats).

"To be honest," said Moose Skowron, "we [Yankees players] were hoping that Mickey would break the record because he was in that category [his status as a bona-fide superstar and, for years, the Yankees' leader] to break the record."

*

Skowron, among the most decent, loyal, and humble of men, had gone back farther with Mantle than any other Yankee. They first met in the fall of 1950. Mantle was just 18 years old and was rising rapidly in the Yankees' farm system. He had just completed his second season of professional baseball at Joplin, Missouri, in the Class C Western Association, where he batted .383, hit 26 homers, and drove in 136 runs.

As a reward for his great season, to get a look at him, and to get him accustomed to being around a big-league team, the Yankees brought Mantle on a western road trip in September. Mantle joined the Yankees in St. Louis and got to hit in the batting cage with the extra men and take infield practice (he was a shortstop in those days).

From St. Louis, the Yankees moved to Chicago, where they were joined by another young player, an 18-year-old Chicago kid who had just signed a contract with the Yankees. He had been a punter at Purdue, and a pretty good one, but baseball was his first love and he believed it was his future. The kid's name was William Joseph Skowron, but everyone called him "Moose," a nickname he acquired from a family member who saw a resemblance between young Skowron and the Italian dictator Benito Mussolini.

After Chicago, Mantle and Skowron got to accompany the team to New York and work out at Yankee Stadium. In the Bronx, the two young players roomed together at the Concourse Plaza Hotel, within walking distance of Yankee Stadium. It was the beginning of a close friendship that would last until Mantle's death 45 years later.

Despite their close friendship, Skowron rarely socialized with Mantle.

"Mickey and Whitey [Ford] would ask me to go out with them, but I wouldn't go," said Skowron. "Mickey would ask me, 'Moose, don't you like me?' I said, 'Mickey, I don't live the way you live,' and he respected me for that. But in 1961, after Ralph Houk became manager, we were in spring training and Houk said, 'Moose, you got to do me a favor. You gotta go with these two guys. They want to take you out for dinner.' I said I didn't want to go, but Houk begged me so I said okay.

"I was to be the chauffeur. Mickey and Whitey rented a limousine and they bought me a chauffeur's cap and I drove them around St. Petersburg and Clearwater. Every time we stopped at a bar, I got out of the car and I had to see the manager and say, 'I got Mickey Mantle and Whitey Ford in the back seat.' The managers wouldn't believe me, so I'd tell them to come out to the car and they'd come out and when they saw Mickey and Whitey, they'd say, 'Come on in, have dinner and a couple of drinks.' This went on all night, and we ended up going bowling at 4:30 in the morning.

"That day we had an afternoon game against the Phillies. I figured Houk would give me the day off after

I did him a favor, but my name was on the lineup card. I was taking infield for the game and I said to Houk, 'Ralph, I can't play. I'm seeing two baseballs coming at me.' But Houk said I had to play. I just was going to have to struggle through it. But when the game was about to start, Houk took me out of the lineup and that's when I realized that I had been had. Mickey and Whitey had set the whole thing up with Houk.

"After we were retired, Mickey never stopped thinking of me. He would invite me and Hank Bauer to do card shows with him and to work at the fantasy camp he had with Whitey. When I had my double heart bypass in 1995, Mickey was the last one to call me. I was being rolled in for the operation and I got the call and he said, 'Moose I love you.' I said 'Mickey, I love you, too.' And two months later he died.

"In 1961, Roger asked me to live with him, but I said 'No, Roger, you're living with [Bob] Cerv downtown, and I want to stay in New Jersey.' And then Roger and Cerv got Mickey to move in with them.

"Most of us were pulling for Mickey to break the record, but after Mickey got hurt, then everybody switched to Roger's side and we were pulling for him to break the record. Roger was a hell of a nice guy and he was a great ballplayer. He could run, he broke up double plays, he was a great outfielder, had a great arm. He was a winner. He didn't want to be bothered, but the writers gave him a hard time. He'd go to the bathroom and all the photographers would follow him in there and were taking pictures. He got angry about that. He wanted to be left alone."

*

After hitting home run No. 51, Mantle was in one of his infrequent good moods, and he seemed to be enjoying the banter with the press. He was pleased, Mantle said, that he was getting pitches to hit.

"They're not trying to walk me," he said. "They're still throwing strikes because they know Yogi [Berra] and Ellie [Howard] are hitting behind me."

Someone told Mantle that even if he failed to catch Ruth, he could take heart and make history by pointing to the center-field fence, like Babe did in the 1932 World Series, and hit one there.

"Not me," he laughed. "If I did, I'd probably strike out."

Then Mantle reconsidered. "I'd do it if they put a trap door at home plate. Then if I strike out, they can pull a string and the trap door will open and I'll disappear into the ground."

Perhaps stimulated by the challenge from his teammate and roommate, Maris proved he is nothing if not resourceful by arousing from his batting slump with a bang to once again pose a stern threat to Ruth's record. On September 6, he hit his 54th home run, and on September 7, he hit his 55th as the Yankees stretched their winning streak to eight games and their lead over the second-place Tigers to nine games.

Home runs in consecutive games while Mantle failed to leave the yard gave Maris a lead of four home runs over Mantle and left him seven games ahead of Ruth's record pace.

With the finish line of the season in sight, and the home run record in serious peril, a sudden influx of members of the out of town press began streaming into Yankee Stadium to report on the Yankees' M&M Boys' pursuit of Ruth. They included veteran baseball writers and eager young hopefuls, representatives of established and respected newspapers and magazines, and ambitious amateurs trying to make names for themselves. There was one thing, however, they all had in common with those who had covered the Yankees for the entire season: they would quickly run out of questions to ask.

Such was the case on September 7, the night of Maris' 55th home run. The horde of reporters, notebooks at the ready and pencils poised, huddled around Maris' locker waiting for him to utter some words of wisdom, shed some light on his mission.

There was a lull in the conversation when, at long last, from the back of the pack came a question from a young man who would later reveal he was from Texas and was a freelance writer hoping to crack the big time.

"Roger," he queried, "you're batting .271 this season. You've never batted .300 and everybody knows that's the standard of excellence in baseball. So, tell me, would you rather hit 60 home runs or bat .300?"

"That question takes the cake," said Elson Howard, standing nearby.

"Now I've heard everything," said John Blanchard.

"Which would you rather do?" Maris replied.

"Bat .300," said the young man.

"To each his own," said Maris.

CHAPTER FIFTEEN

Chicago Hope

WITH THE DAYS DWINDLING DOWN to a precious few and the Yankees having all but clinched their 26th American League pennant, all the attention, and the pressure, was on Roger Maris and Mickey Mantle in their race to beat Babe Ruth's record and commissioner Ford Frick's 154-game deadline. Maris stood at 56 home runs, three games ahead of Ruth's pace, while Mantle had 53 homers, two games behind Ruth's pace.

Maris had hit his 56th against Cleveland on September 9. A day later, Mantle also burned the Indians for his 53rd. Together, the M&M Boys had 109 homers, two more than Ruth and Lou Gehrig totaled in 1927 when they set the record for home runs in one season by two teammates.

Now the Yankees were embarking on a grueling and enervating 13-game trip that would take them to Chicago, Detroit, Baltimore, and Boston.

The first stop was Chicago's Comiskey Park, where Maris would be swinging against his favorite patsies, White Sox pitchers—he had hit 13 of his 56 home runs against them, five in Chicago—and where he picked up endorsements from some credible sources.

Ted Williams said in a television interview in Boston that he was "pretty sure" Maris would break Ruth's record. Williams also said he thought Mantle had a good chance to pass Ruth.

Part of the reason for Maris' success, said Williams, was his knack for, "hitting the ball in the air consistently. It's hard to see how a hitter can hit around .270 or .275 and get 140 to 150 hits at most and end up with 60 homers [Maris had 141 hits in 1960 and would end up with a career high of 159 in 1961]. But, apparently, he gets that loft to them more times than any other hitter that swings for homers."

In Chicago, Hank Greenberg was asked to assess the chances of the M&M Boys breaking Ruth's record.

"I think one will, both might, but not in 154 games," said the man who challenged the record in 1938 but hit only two home runs in his final nine games and finished with 58. Greenberg, like Roger Maris and Henry Aaron after him, had been the recipient of hate mail and death threats. In his case it was due to vitriolic, hateful, and unconscionable anti-Semitism.

"I had five games to go and only two homers to hit and I should have done it," Greenberg said. "Mainly, it was the pressure. Not only was the pressure on me, it was on the pitchers, too. It was the same pressure that now is on Maris and Mantle. It's the tension. You fear time is running out. You become impatient. You become paralyzed at the plate. You're so fearful that you're going to swing at a bad pitch you wind up taking a good one. Then you become so disgusted with yourself you start swinging at the bad pitches.

"If I were Maris or Mantle, I'd forget the 154-game ruling and concentrate on hitting 61 homers in 162 games. If either breaks the record after the deadline set by the commissioner, who's going to deny them the honor?"

Ralph Kiner, who twice chased the record with 51 in 1947 and 54 in 1949, said, "I think Maris has only a slim chance to break the record in 154 games, Mantle none, but I think both will do it in 162, and if that happens, the record will be recognized by the fans."

Said Al Kaline: "Whoever hits 61 is entitled to the record, no matter how many games it takes. It was the owner and leagues who told us how many games to play, not the players."

In the first game of the their rugged 13-game trip, the Yankees beat the White Sox 4–3 for their 13th straight win in a game shortened to six innings by rain. Mantle struck out, flied to center, and singled. Maris walked, took a third strike, singled, and fouled to the first baseman. He complained, not about being rained out of a precious at-bat—"We won, didn't we? That's all that matters. I hope all our games get rained out in the sixth inning, as long as we're ahead"—but about three strike calls by home-plate umpire Hank Soar.

"I didn't get too many strikes, but they were *called* strikes," Maris said. "I was swinging in self-defense. He [Soar] called me out on a swing when I didn't swing. Soar's a better umpire than that. He just had a bad night, I guess. I was trying to lay off the bad pitches, but it didn't do any good. He called them time after time. All I ask [for] is a fair shake. I know they've got a tough job and I never argue with an ump until I'm sure I'm right.

"I realize people will say I'm a crybaby, but I can't help it. Not after the bad calls I got."

"He's so tight, he can't breathe up there," said Soar, a burly former football player who played nine seasons in the National Football League as a running back and defensive back with the New York Giants. In 1938, he caught the game-winning touchdown pass for the Giants against the Green Bay Packers in the NFL Championship Game (before there was a Super Bowl) in the Polo Grounds. "He's trying so hard, he thinks every pitch he leaves alone is a ball. He [Maris] has never said a word to me before. I honestly like him very much. I try not to look at him when he's up. He's just another batter. I look at the plate and the pitch. I figure he's in a spot and the pressure is getting him. They never give him a good pitch to hit. They keep throwing him all that junk, low and inside. I know what he's going through."

Maris' biggest complaint came in the second inning when the Yankees had runners on second and third and one out. He started to bunt, held up, and Soar called him out on strikes.

"He's going for a home run record," said Soar. "What's he bunting for, anyway?"

"I bunted," Maris said, "because we might have needed that other run to win [see August 7]. As it turned out, we almost did. Suppose they scored that run in the sixth, then we would have had a tie. That's why I was going to bunt."

Maris was reminded that the win put the Yankees 11½ games ahead with only 17 games to play, practically an insurmountable lead.

"I feel we've got it [the pennant]," Maris said. "But I want to make sure. That's why we've been fighting for, what, 145 games? Suppose we went on a 10-game losing streak!"

The rain continued the following day and the second game between the Yankees and White Sox was called off after two-and-a-half innings. It would be made up as a doubleheader the following day. It meant the Yankees would be playing back-to-back doubleheaders within 48 hours, two against the White Sox on September 14, and then a plane trip to Detroit where they would play a doubleheader on September 15.

On September 14, American League president Joe Cronin, at odds with commissioner Ford Frick's ruling, proclaimed his belief that a player hitting 61 home runs at any stage of a 162-game season should be recognized as having set the record. Cronin, by coincidence, was a contemporary of Ruth as a player, a Hall of Famer, and a .301 lifetime hitter with three teams, the Pittsburgh Pirates, Washington Senators, and Boston Red Sox and a pennant-winning manager with the Senators and Red Sox. His playing record having dated back to Ruth's day made him an exception to the trend of old-time baseball players (i.e., Ty Cobb and Rogers Hornsby) who were eager to protect Ruth's record and legacy. Cronin's position in the controversy, however, may have been dictated by what he deemed was in the best financial interest of his league.

Informed of Cronin's comments, Frick told the Associated Press, "You don't break the 100-meter record in the 100-yard dash." Frick then reiterated—again without uttering the word "asterisk"—"There'll be two records, the most home runs in a 162-game schedule and the most home runs in a 154-game schedule."

True to their previous comments, Maris and Mantle refused to be drawn into the controversy.

"I'd like to do it in 154 games," said Maris, "but I'll be proud of whatever I get."

Said Mantle: "It really doesn't matter to me although all along I've said only 154 games should be recognized."

In 1958, the commissioner and the two league presidents had authorized the formation of a Major League Records Committee that was empowered to vote on the approval of all records. Serving on the committee were Dave Grote, public relations director of the National League; Joe McKenney, public relations director of the American League; Seymour Siwoff of the Elias Sports Bureau; and veteran baseball writers Cliff Kachline of *The Sporting News,* John Drebinger of the *New York Times,* Dan Daniel of the *New York World Telegram & Sun,* and Joe Reichler of the Associated Press.

The committee was scheduled to meet in December, at which time the key issue under discussion was almost certain to be the home run record controversy.

Said one member of the committee: "I don't care which way we vote, so long as we vote."

In the doubleheader in Chicago on September 14, Maris and Mantle confirmed baseball wisdom that has long held the belief that it's harder to win two games in one day than to win games on two separate days and because fatigue sets in, hitters are usually not as effective in a doubleheader as they are in two single games.

In the first game of the doubleheader, Maris had two hits, both singles, in four trips. Mantle was 0–4. In the second game, Maris struck out, popped to third, flied to center, and singled. Mantle popped to first, flied to right, walked, and grounded into a force-out.

The Yankees hit one home run in the doubleheader, by Elston Howard. It was the Yankees 220th of the season, leaving them one short of the major league record set by the 1947 New York Giants and tied by the 1956 Cincinnati Reds. That was one record that was certain to fall, and no asterisk would be needed.

In the three-game series, Maris and Mantle combined for 23 plate appearances and failed to hit a home run, surprising because of how they had punished White Sox pitchers all season. Their failure to hit a home run in the three games was a serious blow to their chances of catching Ruth.

Maris was now only one game ahead of Ruth's pace. Mantle, however, fell five games behind and was ready to toss in the towel.

"I can't make it," Mantle conceded. "Not even in 162 games. I figured if I could have hit a couple here, I might have been able to do it. But I don't think I can do it now. I just didn't hit a ball good all day."

Said Maris: "The wind [gusts of up to 25 miles per hour blowing out to right field] favored a pull hitter like me, but I didn't really get under the ball in either game [he lifted three balls in the air in eight at-bats, a pop to third and two flies to shallow center]."

"Just because they go four or five games without hitting a homer, everybody thinks they're pressing or in a slump," said manager Ralph Houk. "Hell, it's not the first time they went that many games without hitting one. They might hit four in tomorrow's doubleheader [against the Tigers]. It wouldn't surprise me."

CHAPTER SIXTEEN

Brotherly Love

DESPITE FAILING TO HIT A HOME RUN in three games in Chicago, Roger Maris arrived in Detroit in a good mood, cheered by the arrival in town of his older brother, Rudy, who had driven in from North Dakota. As Maris prepared for a twi-night doubleheader against the Tigers, he chatted amiably with reporters.

Maris said he was surprised to learn that Mantle, his partner in mayhem, had tossed in the towel on his chances of breaking Babe Ruth's single-season home run record. What's more, said Maris, he could not agree with his pal's assessment of the situation.

"Mickey is too good a hitter, too great a competitor to have conceded," he said. "I don't think he's out of it at all. No sir. I don't count myself out, and I can't count out Mickey. I may not do a thing here over the weekend, but I'm going to keep on thinking I may break the record until I have exhausted every chance."

Several hours later, after the Yankees and Tigers had split the doubleheader and Maris had had an atrocious day (he had one hit, a single, in nine at-bats, struck out twice, grounded out twice, reached on an error, and flied out three times), his mood changed. He refused to talk with reporters and took refuge from them in the trainer's room, which is the players' sanctuary, off-limits to the media.

In most stadiums the trainer's room is in the rear of the clubhouse, out of sight. In Tiger Stadium it was in the middle of the room, separated by a metal grating. Consequently, Maris could run, but he could not hide. He was visible to all, seen conversing with his brother in plain view of impatient working reporters on deadline.

Maris had sent word through Yankees' director of public relations Bob Fishel, who reported that Maris said, "From now on I'm going in the trainer's room. They've been ripping me everywhere I go."

Fishel quickly pointed out that Maris was not talking about being "ripped" in New York. "But out of town they've been rough on him."

With the clock ticking and deadlines approaching, one reporter took his case to manager Ralph Houk, who wondered, "What could he say if he did come out?"

The reporter told Houk it was unfair that a player could escape to an area where the press was not allowed.

"Don't tell me where I can allow people," Houk roared.

"But his brother is in there," the reporter persisted.

Now Houk was riled. "Don't tell me his brother can't go in there," he bellowed. "That's the most ridiculous thing I've heard. I wish that was the only problem I had. He didn't hit a home run. He hit one single, he wore the same pair of shoes, the same glove, he broke one bat, and cussed out one fan. There's the whole story. I gave it to you."

Shortly thereafter, Maris left the trainer's room and headed for his locker. "I have nothing to say," he commented with a wave.

"Were you hiding?" someone asked.

"No. I always sit in the trainer's room after a game in Detroit," he said. "Ask anyone. If I want to stay in there, I'll stay in there. I have nothing to say."

"Do you still think you have a chance for the record?"

"What record?" he replied.

"Babe Ruth's record."

"Am I close to it? I don't want to talk about it. If you want me to concede, I'll concede."

Maris had gone 27 at-bats without a home run. He was stuck at 56 and was now tied with Ruth's record pace as the clock kept ticking.

By contrast, Mantle, who was 2-for-5 with a single and a double, three walks, and one RBI in the doubleheader but was mired in a 3-for-17 slump, hadn't hit a home run in 18 at-bats and had fallen four games behind the record pace, was uncharacteristically effusive after the games. Perhaps it was Mantle's way of filling the role of leader by deflecting attention and criticism away from Maris.

"I had a lot of good balls to hit tonight," Mantle said. "I hit some of them good, too, but I didn't get enough lift. I want to know how the Tigers got Ronnie Kline [who held the Yankees to seven hits and pitched a complete game in the Tigers' 4–2 win in the second game] out of the National League. He looks like a good pitcher to me."

Mantle remained pessimistic about his chances of breaking the record within the 154-game span.

"Am I going to hit eight homers in five games?" he asked rhetorically. "How many times has that been done? Sure, if I hit four tomorrow, I've still got a chance. But [Frank] Lary is pitching and he ain't gonna be throwing them up underhanded. I'm lucky to get a single off him. I'm not counting myself out in 162 games, but it'll be tough."

Mantle was right. He was lucky to get a single off Lary. It came with the Tigers ahead 10–3 in the eighth inning after Mantle had flied to right, struck out looking, and struck out swinging. (Mantle also was being characteristically humble. He would have 138 official at-bats against Lary in his career, more than any other pitcher except Early Wynn and Billy Pierce, and he would bat a respectable .297 against him with nine home runs and 24 RBIs.) Detroit would go on to win 10–4 and Lary would pitch a complete game and improve his career record against the Yankees to 27–10.

Maris, on the other hand, broke out of his slump and ended his home run drought when he solved Lary for a two-run homer, his 57th, in the third inning that tied the score 2–2. The ball hit against the right-field roof, some 370' away from home plate and 82' high, and bounced back onto the playing field where it was retrieved by Tigers' right fielder Al Kaline, who tossed it into the Yankees' dugout.

After the game, Detroit writers asked Maris how he felt about Kaline's thoughtful gesture of retrieving the ball for him.

"Any player would do the same thing," said Maris, a remark that got him criticized in Detroit newspapers the following day for failing to properly acknowledge the considerate gesture of Kaline, a Detroit idol.

"Roger needed a home run today," Mantle said. "He got it, and I think it will give him a big lift. I also think he has a helluva shot at the record. If he can get another one tomorrow, I think he'll be in position to do it [break Ruth's record within the 154-game limit] in the first three games in Baltimore."

"That was a big one for Roger," said manager Houk. "Psychologically, it should do him a world of good. He hadn't hit one since last Saturday and he was aware of that, too. Maybe that was getting him down. Now he might have found the groove again. He's the type of hitter who can get hot suddenly and stay hot for a long stretch."

The following day, Mantle's chances of breaking the record appeared at an end when he was hitless in four official at-bats (he walked twice), making him 4-for-25 and homerless in 25 at-bats. Against Jim Bunning, Maris walked in the first inning, struck out in the third, and walked again in the fifth. In the seventh, he batted with two outs and Tony Kubek, who had singled, on first. Maris drove a wicked line drive to right-center that missed clearing the fence by inches. The ball bounced off the wall and rattled around as Maris circled the bases with a triple that scored Kubek and gave the Yankees a 4–2 lead.

The Tigers tied the score with two in the bottom of the eighth and the game went into extra innings, a fortuitous reprieve for Maris. He flied out to center in the 10th inning, but got another chance in the 12th. Maris came to bat again with Kubek on first and drove home run No. 58 against the facing of the upper right-field stands, a tremendous blast 400' away, to give the Yankees a 6–4 victory. He had now hit more home runs than any player in history except Babe Ruth (Jimmie Foxx in 1932 and Hank Greenberg in 1938 also hit 58).

"Even if I don't do another thing in baseball, I've at least got one year that puts me in a pretty good class," Maris said. "Even if I never do anything else, I can always say I was second to Babe Ruth."

Maris admitted that hitting 58 home runs was his greatest thrill and "more than I ever expected when I started in this game. You always feel good after a home run, but this felt especially good because it won the game. Just because I was fortunate to hit that one, you've got 25 happy guys here," he said, as he gestured around the clubhouse, "plus a couple of coaches and a manager."

Somebody mentioned to Maris that he seemed very matter-of-fact for someone who had just reached a tremendous baseball milestone.

"Sure, I was aware I tied two guys with that one," he said, "but you don't lose your head over a thing like that. Maybe I'll get excited if I'm fortunate to hit 60."

His home run had come in the Yankees' 152nd game, including one tie. In 1927, Babe Ruth had hit two in the Yankees' 153rd game, including one tie. They came on September 29 in a 15–4 defeat of the Washington Senators. He hit No. 58 off Hod Lisenbee and No. 59 off Paul Hopkins. Ruth also hit a triple and drove in six runs.

Ruth's 60th came on September 30 against Tom Zachary and the Senators in the Yankees' 154th game. In game No.

155, Ruth would go hitless in three at-bats against Bobby Burke and Garland Braxton of the Senators.

Roger Maris had come down to the final three games in a 154-game schedule, needing two home runs to tie Ruth's record and three to pass it. And he'd have to do it in the city of Babe Ruth's birth, Baltimore, where he had not hit a home run all season.

Chapter Seventeen

Mantle Quits

Mickey Mantle had a cold! Chills…fever…the works. He ached all over. He was weak. He felt like sleeping all the time.

Monday, September 18, was an off-day, the quiet before the storm, four games in three days against the Orioles in Baltimore, games No. 152, 153, 154, and 155 for the Yankees, not including the one tie.

Mantle spent the off-day sleeping. Maris spent it relaxing, reflecting, and complaining (again). Each day, he said, is a carbon copy of the previous day, filled with the badgering of hopeful interviewers, ubiquitous photographers, and relentless autograph seekers.

"People are beginning to recognize me," Maris said. "Sometimes that's not so good."

"They spotted him in church [Sunday] in Detroit," said Bob Cerv, his friend, teammate, and roommate. "They waited for him after Mass and got him coming out. He must have signed 100 autographs."

Although he often was accommodating and courteous to fans, he was growing intolerant with gossip columnists, most of whom never showed up at Yankee Stadium and had never even met Maris, such as the one that reported Roger had taken actress Ava Gardner to dinner.

"Cerv and my friend Big Julie took me to dinner on my birthday [September 10] and she [Ava Gardner] was there," Maris explained. "I did meet her, but that's all there was to it, but they made it look like I was alone with her. I'm too much in love with my wife to do anything like that."

In Detroit, Maris had mentioned, perhaps in jest, that he was thinking about asking manager Ralph Houk to give him a day off in Baltimore.

"He hasn't said anything to me about it," said Houk. "I assume he'll be in the lineup tomorrow night."

If he ever was serious about it, Maris had changed his mind—or had it changed for him. Presumably wiser heads, more aware than he of the magnitude of the record he was chasing and more understanding of the working of the New York media and the minds of the New York sports fans, convinced Maris that taking a day off would be a colossal mistake.

"I won't ask for a rest," he said. "Not now."

*

Maris had agreed to meet on the off-day in Baltimore with Milton Gross, sports columnist for the *New York Post* who was working on a magazine article about the Yankees' home run slugger, but when he arrived in town, Maris got a call from his old friend, Whitey Herzog. They had been teammates in Kansas City, and they lived near each other in Raytown. Now, Herzog was winding down an eight-year journeyman playing career with the Orioles.

Herzog asked Maris if he would accompany him to a local hospital to visit the son of a friend who was dying of leukemia. Maris said he would, on one condition: that there would be no publicity of his visit.

Herzog agreed and arranged to pick Maris up at the Yankees' hotel and drive him to the hospital. In so doing, Maris forgot about agreeing to meet with Gross. When Maris failed to show for the appointment, Gross told Yankees officials that he was determined to "destroy" Maris because of the slight.

Meanwhile, because Herzog was a close friend and had been for years, Maris felt he had a sounding board to vent his frustrations, which he did on the drive to the hospital. He confided to Herzog that he was near the breaking point. The press was hounding him, the photographers were dogging him, the fans were harassing him. He couldn't walk across the lobby of the hotel or get on the team bus without being mobbed. To alleviate some of the stress and get some peace and quiet, Herzog suggested Maris move in with Herzog and his wife for a day or two while he was in Baltimore, and Maris accepted.

The day off did not help Mantle, who felt worse the next day yet still showed up for the doubleheader. He took a penicillin shot but was too sick to play.

"That's it, Rog, I'm through," he told Maris. "It's all up to you now."

Mantle did come to bat as a pinch-hitter in the ninth inning of the first game and was struck out by Steve Barber for the final out of a 1–0 victory by the Orioles.

"Sure I wanted to break Babe Ruth's record," Mantle said years later. "Who wouldn't? But if I couldn't do it, I was hoping Roger would. And when I got hurt late in the season and knew I no longer had a shot at the record, I was pulling for Roger to do it as much as anybody."

A crowd of 31,317 showed up at Memorial Stadium, most of them there to support Maris, and if they would not openly root for him, they at least could witness his historic bid to break the record of their native son, Babe Ruth. They attended despite the fact that Hurricane Esther was beginning to gather her full fury and was blowing hard from right field into the face of the batters.

The crowd booed when Maris walked in his first time at-bat, their ire aimed directly at the hometown's starting pitcher, Steve Barber, a 23-year-old, second-year, hard-throwing lefthander who had won 16 games, seven of them by shutout. In the third inning, Maris hit a lazy foul pop-up to the first baseman, Jim Gentile. In the sixth, he grounded out to Gentile unassisted. In the eighth, his drive to right field was held up by the wind—or by the baseball gods— and caught by Orioles right fielder Earl Robinson.

Game two of the doubleheader was a makeup of the April 22 game that had been called because of rain in the bottom of the seventh inning with the score tied 5–5—a game in which both Mantle and Maris had home runs washed away. Mantle did not start, and Maris shifted from right field to center but remained in the No. 3 batting position. Yogi Berra batted fourth and played left field.

Against the Orioles' starter, Hal (Skinny) Brown, a 36-year-old, 11-year-veteran knuckleball pitcher, Maris hit a pop foul to first in the first inning, reached on an infield hit in the third, grounded out to third baseman Brooks Robinson in the fourth, and hit a high, lazy fly to center in the seventh after getting out in front of Brown's knuckleball and driving it on a line into the right-field seats but foul.

He came to bat for the last time in the ninth and faced another knuckleball pitcher, future Hall of Famer Hoyt Wilhelm. Maris took one pitch outside for a ball and then swung futilely at three tantalizing knuckleballs, missing all three.

Maris always did have trouble hitting the knuckleball and, in Brown and Wilhelm, the Orioles had two of the best in the business. To Roger's chagrin he had to face not one, but both of them in critical game No. 153. He still needed three more home runs to break Babe Ruth's record, and he had only one more game to do it, according to the Frick doctrine.

"Do you think you can hit three in one game?" Maris was asked.

"You'd be almost a Houdini if you did it," Maris said.

"As far as Mr. Frick's concerned, I've got only one more game. As far as I'm concerned, my body has to go out there nine more times...154 or 162...I'm not going to worry about it. I'm going to do the best I can."

CHAPTER EIGHTEEN

Ill Wind

WEDNESDAY, SEPTEMBER 20, 1961, was the day of reckoning for Roger Maris; the day by which he would have to pass Babe Ruth's record of 60 home runs to be proclaimed baseball's all-time single-season home run champion or forever be an asterisk.

By every measure, Maris was faced with a nearly impossible task. He would have to hit three home runs in that night's game, something he had never done in his career; he would have to hit them in Baltimore, the city of Babe Ruth's birth; he would have to hit them in Memorial Stadium, where the only home run he hit all season was wiped out when a rainstorm forced the game to be canceled; and he had to do all that while facing a gale force wind blowing in from right field to home plate.

Maris had spent the night at the home of his pal Whitey Herzog, who drove him to the ballpark and left him with one parting admonition. "I hope you hit three home runs tonight and we win the game 4–3."

As was his custom, Maris was one of the first to arrive in the Yankees' clubhouse, several hours before game time. He was nervous and jumpy, the time hanging on him like an albatross. Unable to sit, he spent the time smoking and pacing, pacing and smoking.

"I knew if I sat down in front of my locker for long, my stomach would end up in a hundred knots," he said. "I kept picking up things and looking at them. I wanted to keep my hands busy."

He had hoped to kill some time taking batting practice, a regular pregame routine he found relaxing and important to his preparation, but it was raining and batting practice was canceled. So Maris continued to smoke and pace, pace and smoke.

The rain stopped in time for the game to start on schedule with a crowd of 21,032 on hand, some 10,000 fewer than the previous day, the attendance held down perhaps by the weather or by the realization that Maris was up against so great an obstacle that there would be no record set this night.

One thing in Maris' favor was the Orioles' choice to be their starting pitcher, 12-game-winner Milt Pappas, a hard-throwing right-hander with a live fastball and a good curve, the type of pitcher Maris had feasted on. He had hit two home runs off Pappas but none this year. Ralph Terry was the starting pitcher for the Yankees.

Pat Maris, Roger's wife, watched the game on television from a studio in Kansas City.

Claire Ruth, Babe's widow, watched from her Riverside Drive apartment.

Commissioner Ford Frick watched from his home in Bronxville, New York, an upscale suburb of Manhattan.

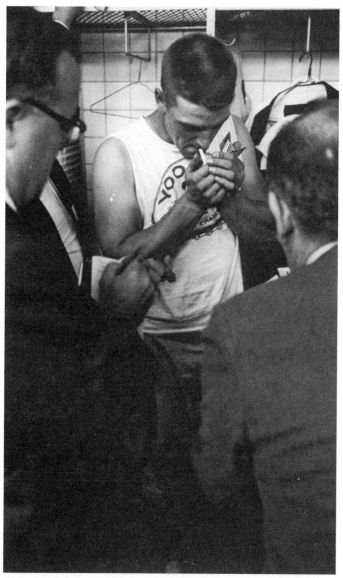

Roger Maris lights up as he prepares to meet the press at his Yankee Stadium locker after a game in 1961, his record year. (PHOTO BY ART RICKERBY//TIME LIFE PICTURES/GETTY IMAGES)

Leading off for the Yankees, Bobby Richardson reached on an error by second baseman Jerry Adair. Tony Kubek flied out to center field. As Maris strode to the plate for his first at-bat, players from both teams stood up and moved to the top step of the dugout. Maris got into a pitch from Pappas and rocketed it on a line to right field.

"He nailed it," said Terry. "But right into the teeth of that wind in right. On a normal day, it's outta there."

Orioles right fielder Earl Robinson caught the drive a few feet in front of the wall.

The Yankees scored a run in the second on a triple by Moose Skowron and an RBI single by Clete Boyer to take a 1–0 lead. Maris came to bat with one out in the third. With the count in his favor at two balls and one strike and believing that Pappas did not want to walk him, Maris looked for a fastball and got it, driving the pitch high and far toward right field. It cut through the wind, cleared the 14' right-field wall, and carried over the 380' marker into the bleachers.

"I could hear the guys in the dugout yelling for me," Roger said. "When I hit it, I knew it was out, wind or no wind. I hit it square, but I got under it enough so I knew it was gone."

In the right-field stands, a 32-year-old unemployed Baltimorean and a devout Orioles fan named Robert Reitz caught the ball and was taken immediately to the Yankees' clubhouse by Memorial Stadium security and an Orioles front-office executive. Reitz was going to meet Maris. He arrived with an agenda. He posed for pictures with Maris, who assumed the man was there to give him the ball. Roger offered a brand-new autographed baseball in exchange. Reitz declined.

"You gonna keep that?" Maris asked.

Reitz nodded.

"Good luck to you," said Maris, and headed back to the dugout.

Others tried to seduce Reitz with a variety of offers: two autographed baseballs, two tickets for each of the first two World Series games at Yankee Stadium. Reitz remained adamant. He had heard on the radio that someone had offered $2,500 for the ball.

"I don't know what I'm going to do," Reitz told the *New York Times*. "I'm confused. I'm an Orioles fan and I usually sit in the grandstand. But nobody gives me nothing. Would I have asked for money if Jim Gentile would've hit one and I'd caught it? You crazy or something? I wouldn't take anything from Gentile. He's my man."

No deal ever was struck between Reitz and Maris, and the Baltimore fan was never heard from again. The baseball Maris hit for his 59th home run has never surfaced.

Now Maris was one home run away from tying the record, two away from breaking it, and he was certain to get at least two more swings, maybe three. The "impossible" still was possible.

Berra had followed Maris' home run with a homer of his own, after which John Blanchard singled and Elston Howard doubled him home to boost the Yankees' lead to 4–0 and knock Pappas from the game. He was replaced by Dick Hall, nicknamed "Turkey" because he was a tall, gangly right-hander with an awkward herky-jerk sidearm delivery that made it difficult for the batter to pick up the flight of the ball.

When he came to bat in the fourth inning, Maris said to Orioles catcher Gus Triandos, "You think my ass is tight now?" He then settled in the batter's box to face Hall. The count went to 0–2, and Maris pulled the next pitch foul into the right-field stands. Hall then threw a high, hard one up and away to the left-handed hitter. It might have been out of the strike zone, but it was close enough for Maris to hack at it and too close to let it go. He swung viciously… and missed. Strike three!

Terry took his 4–0 lead into the bottom of the sixth when the Orioles put together three singles (they would get only four hits in the game), a walk, and an error to score two runs and cut the Yankees' lead to 4–2.

In the seventh inning, Maris faced Hall again. He was ready, having had one at-bat to gauge Hall's velocity and recognize his pitching pattern. He put a good swing on one pitch and drove it on a wicked line into the right-field seats, but it hooked foul by a good 10'. On Hall's next pitch, Maris squared up the ball and sent it soaring high and far toward the right-field seats. This time, there was no question of fair or foul. The only question was, would it be able to push through the wind?

The answer came when Earl Robinson retreated to the warning track, settled under the ball, and caught it with his back practically against the wall.

"The damn ball just died," Maris said.

If the fates had been kinder to Roger Maris, he could have already had his three home runs in the game—a ball held up by the wind in the first inning, a home run in the third, a ball into the stands that hooked foul in the seventh, and on the next pitch another one held up by the wind—achieved the 'impossible" and become baseball's all-time single-season home run champion, no asterisk required.

It looked like he was done. But when the Yankees, as if bearing down to give their teammate one more chance, put two runners on base in the eighth, it meant Maris would get another chance. He would be the third Yankee to bat in the top of the ninth.

When the Yankees came to bat in the ninth, standing on the mound was Maris' worst nightmare. The new Orioles pitcher was the knuckleball guru himself, Hoyt Wilhelm, who had pitched the ninth inning of the second game the night before and had made Maris look foolish waving at three knuckleballs and missing all three. It was a surprising choice because, with the Yankees still leading 4–2 it was not a save situation for Wilhelm.

"It just wasn't fair," Herzog said. "There was no reason to use Hoyt, other than to make it tough on Roger. They just didn't want Roger to set the record in Ruth's hometown. I'm convinced of that."

Wilhelm later revealed that he was sitting in the Baltimore bullpen in the seventh inning when the telephone rang. It was Orioles manager Luman Harris.

"He told me to warm up because I was going to pitch the ninth," Wilhelm said. "I knew I would face Roger. I had plenty of time to get ready, and my adrenaline was flowing as much for that game as any game I've ever pitched in.

"I would have liked to see Roger get the record—we had played together in Cleveland and I thought he was a good guy. But I didn't want Roger to get it off me. No pitcher wants to go into the record book like that. But I also didn't want to walk him. Roger deserved a shot at the record."

Wilhelm's first pitch, a knuckleball, was taken for strike one. His next pitch, another knuckleball, started out high and outside and then took a left turn and headed down and in. Maris started to swing and then tried to stop his swing. The ball hit his bat and trickled toward first base. Wilhelm got off the mound quickly and picked up the ball. Maris, dejected, stood frozen at home plate for an instant, and then he began jogging lazily toward first base, carrying his bat with him. Wilhelm, the ball in his glove, met Maris in front of first base and tagged him gently.

Maris tossed away his bat and jogged out to his position in center field. As he did, he passed the veteran umpire Charlie Berry, who said, "You gave it a good try, son."

John Blanchard, playing right field alongside Maris, carried Roger's glove out to center field and told Maris he was proud to be on the same team with him.

It was over. Roger Maris had finished his season of 154 decisions with 59 home runs, more than any other player in baseball history except the mighty Babe Ruth.

Terry retired the Orioles in order in the bottom of the ninth, and the Yankees had clinched the 26th pennant in their history. The victory celebration in the clubhouse was raucous but bittersweet. There was joy over winning the pennant and disappointment for teammate Maris, who had come so close in his personal quest.

The reaction of the media ranged from those who applauded Maris' effort in the face of such excruciating pressure, to old-time sportswriters like Fred Lieb, who went back to Ruth's day and echoed the sentiment of his generation when he wrote, "Perhaps it may sound corny, but my biggest sports thrill of 1961 was seeing Roger Maris hit a weak squib to Hoyt Wilhelm.... It wasn't that this writer had anything against Maris, but as one of the Old Guard who had been close to Ruth and who had sent word of the 60th homer over the AP wires, one can't be blamed for having nostalgic memories and rooting for the good old Babe."

In Kansas City, a disappointed Pat Maris was close to tears. Sadly, but resignedly, she said, "There's always next year."

Reached at her Riverside Drive apartment, Claire Ruth said, "That was one record I didn't want broken. I have the highest regard for Roger Maris. He is a fine hitter. But the Babe loved that record and he wanted to be known as the king of home runs forever."

There was no comment from Ford Frick.

In the Yankees' clubhouse, Maris removed himself from the pennant-clinching celebration to meet with the assembled media at his locker. He was disappointed but relieved. For the first time all day, he seemed at ease.

"I tried," he declared, "but I didn't quite get it. Although I got only one, I'm very happy and lucky to get what I did. I feel relieved, very relieved. Now that it's over with, I'll try to get straightened out for the World Series. There was a little pressure there."

Speaking of his final at-bat, Maris said, "I was a little disappointed. If I was going to make an out, I at least wanted to make it swinging. That Wilhelm's a pretty tough pitcher to hit."

Maris was asked how he felt about Frick's ruling that, even if he hit more than 60 home runs in the remainder of his season, it would come with an asterisk.

"He's making the rules," Maris said. "I've got nothing to say about it. I'd like to have had it in 154, but that's the breaks of the game. I'm lucky to get where I got. I have no complaints whatever."

What Maris did have was eight more games in which to hit two more home runs and become baseball's all-time single-season home run champion, even if it meant the record would come with an asterisk.

CHAPTER NINETEEN

Hair-Raising

AT FIRST, ROGER MARIS THOUGHT LITTLE of it when he noticed strands of hair in the basin of his bathroom sink, but in the days before the Yankees' 155th game—and commissioner Frick's deadline for being credited with breaking Babe Ruth's cherished record—Maris was growing more and more alarmed. Instead of strands of hair, he was seeing first tufts and then clumps, and now visible were patches of bald spots peeking through his blond crew cut.

Maris brought his concern to trainer Gus Mauch, who reported the condition to the team's public relations director Bob Fishel. It was determined that, on the day after the critical 155th game, Maris, accompanied by Fishel, would be checked out by a local physician in downtown Baltimore.

"I was worried," Maris admitted. "I thought I might have some kind of disease."

The Baltimore physician allayed his fears with several tests that proved negative. He could find nothing physically wrong with Maris. His diagnosis was that the bald patches were the result of stress and nervous tension because of the home run chase, a normal consequence.

"I'm just nervous, that's all," said Maris, his legs jiggling reflexively, as he sat in front of his locker prior to the final game of a four-game series with the Orioles.

For Maris, the "day after" had been a full one. In addition to a visit to the doctor, he had agreed to a meeting arranged by a Baltimore television station at the home of the man who caught his 59th home run. Originally, in exchange for the ball, the man, Robert Reitz, had asked for two tickets to each game of the World Series with all expenses paid for travel and lodging. The Yankees had offered $25.

"We won't even keep the ball," said Fishel. "The Hall of Fame wants it."

When he arrived at Reitz's home, Maris learned that the price for the ball had jumped to $2,500. Maris turned around and left. "I'm not going to let him hold me up," he said.

✳

In New York, Commissioner Frick had ended his silence on the subject of Maris and the asterisk when reporters sought him out for comment. He reiterated his stance that if Maris passes Ruth's record of 60 home runs in his final eight games, it will go into the books as the record for home runs in a season for a 162-game schedule but would not be considered to have broken Ruth's record. Ruth's name will remain on the books for having hit 60 home runs in a 154-game season.

Frick further said there would be no star, or asterisk, next to either Maris' name or Ruth's name that could be construed as disparaging either record.

"My position today is the same as it has been when I first made my ruling," Frick said. "I don't know how I can state it more clearly. If Maris in these remaining games hits 60, 61, or any number of more home runs, that record certainly will go in the book and it will be the record other players will shoot at as long as the 162-game schedule prevails.

"But any such performance made at any time in the future cannot be considered to have broken the Babe Ruth record unless it is made within the 154-game limit.

"As for that star or asterisk business, I don't know how that cropped up or was attributed to me, because I never said it. I certainly never meant to belittle Maris' feat should he wind up with more than 60. Both names will appear in the books as having set records but under different conditions."

Frick also made it clear that his ruling on Ruth's record would also be applied to other season records such as most hits, doubles, triples, and strikeouts. He further emphasized that one of the reasons he took this stand was his belief that the 162-game schedule was only a temporary arrangement adopted by the American League when it expanded from eight to 10 teams and to be followed by the National League when it expanded to 10 teams in 1962.

"I have every reason to believe that if baseball follows its present trend of expansion we'll be back to 154 games within the next five or six years, maybe sooner," Frick said. "This would happen as soon as four more cities acquire major league status.

"In that event, regardless of whether the four new clubs are absorbed to make two 12-club leagues or are combined with two from each of the present two leagues to form a third major league, I am certain we would go back to the 154-game schedule. All are pretty much agreed that the 162-game schedule is unwieldy, but under the present 10-club setup there isn't much of an alternative.

"It therefore would be very unfair to wipe out season records set in the 154-game schedule, which has prevailed for more than 60 years, with those made in 162 games. Why, that could freeze records for years after we return to the 154-game schedule."

Frick left the office of Baseball Commissioner in November 1965, and his prediction of further expansion in baseball came true four years later when both the American and National Leagues increased to 12 teams.

In 1978, the American League expanded to 14 teams. Fifteen years later, the National League also became a 14-team league, and the year after that, both leagues increased from two divisions to three. Through all the expansion and realignment, the schedule never did revert to 154 games. Simply, the owners would not hear of it. Having an additional eight games tacked on to their schedule (and to their turnstile count), they were not about to give them back.

*

The calm after the 154-game storm produced predictable results when the Yankees faced the Orioles with what amounted to the junior varsity on the night after they clinched their 26th American League pennant. Some regulars were hungover from the previous night's victory party. Others were allowed to nurse minor bumps and bruises. Still others were simply given a day of rest.

Bill Skowron, Yogi Berra, Elston Howard, and Clete Boyer did not play. Mickey Mantle was still recuperating from the flu. Bob Hale replaced Skowron at first base. Billy Gardner took over Boyer's third-base position. John Blanchard caught. Hector Lopez was in left field. Jack Reed was in right.

Bobby Richardson led off the game, drew a walk, and was replaced by Joe DeMaestri when the Yankees took the field in the bottom of the second. Rookie Tom Tresh batted third and played shortstop in place of Tony Kubek, who entered the game as a pinch-hitter in the eighth inning and hit a home run. Only Roger Maris among the regulars, batting fourth and playing center field, started and played the entire game, but he played it as if sleepwalking, slogging through nine innings lethargically, seemingly uninterested, fatigued, and distracted.

But there was still the home run record to pursue, so Maris played and did nothing against Jack Fisher—strikeout in the first, lazy fly ball to center in the fourth, ground ball to the first baseman in the seventh, and fly ball to left field in the ninth—who pitched a complete game, allowed three hits, struck out six, and won his 10th game 5–3.

"I wore a size-four collar tonight," Maris said. But instead of the frustration and disappointment that he displayed the previous night, this time there was relief in his voice. He sounded fatigued the night before and indicated he might ask manager Ralph Houk for a day off or two. Now, he was uncertain.

"I don't know what I'm gonna do," Maris said. "I might sit out a game or two, but that's up to the manager."

And the manager said there was no chance he would give Maris a day off.

"I don't anticipate taking him out," Houk said. "In fact, from now on they'll all play except for minor ailments. We're going to have enough off days. There's such a thing as too much rest, you know."

Maris was going to get a chance to rest the following day in Boston, an open date on the Yankees' schedule. After that, there would be two games against the Red Sox in Fenway Park and then back home for two with the Orioles and three with the Red Sox, seven games for Maris to hit two home runs and pass Babe Ruth as baseball's all-time single-season home run champion, asterisk or not.

Chapter Twenty

Dr. Feelgood

When the Yankees arrived in Boston, Mickey Mantle told manager Ralph Houk he was ready to get back in the lineup. Houk acquiesced and on the afternoon of Saturday, September 23, he wrote Mantle's name on his lineup card, in his customary cleanup batting position against Red Sox rookie Don Schwall, a 15-game winner.

Felled by a virus, Mantle had not played in four days. He had not hit a home run in 13 days, covering 26 at-bats. He was weak and achy, still not completely recovered from his illness. But he came to bat in the first inning with runners on first and third and one out and drove a pitch deep into the right-field seats for his 54th home run. It was the sort of Herculean effort that contributed to what would become the Mantle legend.

Mantle would fly out to left field in the third inning, strike out in the fifth, and hit a single in the seventh after which he was removed for a pinch runner.

Maris came to bat five times. He reached on an error, walked twice, hit a squibber in front of the plate and was thrown out by the catcher, and singled.

The Yankees won the game 8–3 with Whitey Ford going five innings to record his 25th win, the most games he would ever win in a season and the most for a Yankees pitcher in 27 years.

Mantle would start again the next afternoon, still battling the virus. He failed to get a hit in three at-bats and took himself out of the game after sending Red Sox right fielder Jackie Jensen to the fence for his drive in the sixth inning.

Against Boston ace Bill Monbouquette, who stymied the Yankees on five hits in a 3–1 victory, Maris had one hit in three at-bats—he walked in the first, flied to center in the fourth, singled in the sixth, and flied to left in the eighth—and had now gone three games without hitting a home run since belting No. 59 in Baltimore. In those three games, Maris had walked three times, a fact that did not escape his notice.

"I thought the pressure would be off me after the 154th game, but I was wrong," Maris said. "It's worse than ever now. The way this is going, I've got five games left, and I don't think I'll hit 60 by the end of the season. With the pitches I'm getting, daddy-o, I'll never get it. It'll never happen. When you're close to something, when you're trying to hit one, that's when it's hardest. Now they're [the pitchers] trying to get me to go after bad pitches. You can bet if I hit another one, it's going to be a mistake by the pitcher.

"I don't even think I'll get any in New York the way they're pitching me now. They're going to make it difficult for me."

Maris said that every strike he'd seen in recent days was on the outside corner, away from his power zone. Against Monbouquette, Maris said he saw one good pitch. "And that one I popped to center."

For his part, Monbouquette insisted he didn't pitch Maris any differently than he always had. He thought Maris had some pitches to hit, but the best he could do with them was line a single in the sixth inning.

"What a pitcher thinks is a good pitch and what a hitter thinks is a good one is not always the same," Maris said. "Especially if you're looking for a pitch to hit out of the park."

It was suggested to Maris that perhaps he was missing pitches because he was tired.

"I've been saying all year that I'm tired," he said. "But nobody would believe me."

*

After the second game in Boston, the Yankees flew to New York, where they would close out the season. On the plane ride home, Mantle mentioned to Yankees broadcaster Mel Allen that he felt terrible.

"I have a doctor," Allen said. "He'll give you a shot that will fix you right up."

Mantle was ready to try anything. When the plane landed, Allen placed a call to his doctor friend and made an appointment for Mantle for the following day.

Allen's friend was Dr. Max Jacobson, known to some as Dr. Feelgood. Among his patients were Elizabeth Taylor and President John F. Kennedy. Dr. Jacobson warmly welcomed Mantle to his office in midtown Manhattan, told him to lower his trousers, took a hypodermic needle, stuck it in Mantle's buttocks, and said, "You'll be fine by morning."

By morning, Mantle was not fine. He felt like he was dying. His right hip, the area around where Dr. Jacobson had plunged his needle, had become infected, forming an abscess. Mantle would end up in Lenox Hill hospital where the abscess had to be lanced and drained.

What caused the infection remains a mystery to this day. Some have speculated that the needle used to inject Mantle was contaminated. Others have said that Dr. Feelgood's aim was awry and that he hit bone instead of flesh. Whatever the reason, Mantle's season was over. He would start one more game, on September 26 against Baltimore, but after drawing a walk in his first at-bat he was in such excruciating pain that he had to leave for a pinch runner and would not come to bat again that season.

*

Commissioner Frick had stated that in the interest of fairness a player that hit more than 60 home runs in 1961 would have to do it within 154 games to be acknowledged as having broken Ruth's record. Frick's justification was that in 1961, the American League had a schedule of 162 games so when Ruth set the record in 1927 he had the disadvantage of playing in eight fewer games than were played in 1961.

Mantle's legion of supporters would argue that in 1961 Mickey hit his 54 home runs in only 514 official at-bats, 76 fewer than Maris, and that when Ruth hit his record 60 home runs in 1927, he had 540 official at-bats. How, they wondered, was Frick's pleas for fairness reconciled with those numbers?

CHAPTER TWENTY-ONE

Going Like 60

MONDAY, SEPTEMBER 25, WAS A DAY OFF for the Yankees. Mickey Mantle spent part of it in a doctor's office and the rest of it sleeping. Roger Maris spent it leisurely with his wife, Pat, who had arrived from Raytown for the final games of the season and the upcoming World Series.

There were five games remaining in the season, two against Baltimore and three against Boston—five games for Maris to hit two home runs and become the first man in baseball history to hit more than 60 home runs in a major league season of any length. And all five games would be played in Yankee Stadium, with its cozy and easily reachable right-field wall a mere 296' down the line and where Maris had already blasted 28 home runs that season.

On the night of Tuesday, September 26, Maris would be swinging against Jack Fisher, the Orioles' 22-year-old right-hander who, just five days before in Baltimore, had beaten the Yankees 5–3 and held Maris hitless in four at-bats (a strike-out, a fly-out to center, a ground-out to first, and a fly-out to left).

Among the crowd of 19,401 gathered at Yankee Stadium was Claire Ruth, the Babe's widow, a guest of the Yankees who was seated in a box adjacent to the home team's dugout.

Maris batted in the first inning with two outs and nobody on base and stroked a solid single to center. He came up again in the third. Again there were two outs and nobody on base. Fisher's first pitch was high and tight. Maris turned on it and pulled it into the right-field seats, foul by a good margin. Maris turned to catcher Gus Triandos and said, "Man, can't that guy throw me nothing but jammers?"

Fisher's next pitch was a curveball. Maris chased it and sliced it foul outside third. Maris took the next two pitches for balls, evening the count at 2–2. Thinking Maris might be getting ready to muscle up for a fastball, Fisher threw a curveball. Maris was ready for it. He put a mighty swing on it and the ball soared toward right field, Maris standing motionless at home plate watching the ball sail into the Bronx night. The clock on the Yankee Stadium center-field scoreboard read 8:47.

"I knew it was gone," he said later. "It was just a question of what side of the pole it was gonna stay on. There wasn't much point leaving the batter's box."

Maris didn't need Yankee Stadium's short porch. He didn't need the 45" high fence. He sent Fisher's curveball soaring high and far to right field. It sailed into the third deck, some 6' inside the foul pole and almost 50' off the ground. As it did, Claire Ruth, visibly shaken, left her seat. She would return later. (Veteran sportswriters who had been there 34 years before said Maris' shot landed about 40' to the right of where Ruth hit his 60th home run, into the wooden bleachers of four-year-old Yankee Stadium on September 30, 1927). Maris' ball crashed into an empty seat in the third row and bounced back onto the field where it was picked up by Orioles right fielder Earl Robinson. First-base umpire Ed Hurley asked Robinson for the ball and tossed it to Yankees first base coach Wally Moses, who rolled it to the Yankees' dugout. This time, unlike No. 59 in Baltimore, there would be no fan attempting to extort a pot full of gold from Maris or the Yankees.

"I was glad he hit his 60th," Earl Robinson said, "though I thought for a minute it would go foul. I was glad it bounced back out onto the field so he could get it back. I mean, I know I would like to get that ball if I were in the same situation."

After he saw where the ball came to rest, Maris lowered his head, dropped his bat, and deferentially trotted slowly around the bases.

"I don't remember what my thoughts were," he would say later. "I was in a fog. I still am. I thought I was probably the happiest guy in the world. I was happy when it went in the seats. It's the greatest thing that has ever happened to me, probably the greatest thing that will ever happen to me. I'm just happy and fortunate to have what I have."

As he circled the bases, the crowd was on its feet cheering mightily for the man who had been so reviled throughout the season but who now stood side by side with Babe Ruth as the only players ever to hit 60 home runs in a season. The crowd was still on its feet cheering when Maris reached home and then jogged the few feet to the dugout where he received a congratulatory greeting from his teammates. He ducked into the dugout, but the cheering continued, the crowd imploring him to come out to acknowledge their applause with a curtain call, virtually unprecedented in the glorious history of the big ballpark.

"I really appreciate it," Maris said. "The people, they've been real good to me. I didn't know what to do. I was bewildered. I was never in this spot before.

"Some of the fellows told me to go out, but I thought I might feel sort of silly. I didn't want to do the wrong thing."

Plate umpire Bill Kinnamon beckoned to Maris, and several of his teammates half shoved him to the front of the dugout. Maris appeared, cap in hand, which he waved toward the crowd, embarrassingly accepting the adulation that rained down upon him. Within moments, he had ducked back down into the dugout.

As jubilant as was the reaction of Maris' teammates and the Yankee Stadium crowd, reaction to home run No. 60 was relatively subdued in some quarters. As an example, consider the Associated Press account:

"Roger Maris blasted his 60th homer of the season Tuesday night, but it came four official games too late to officially tie Babe Ruth's 34-year-old record in 154 games."

Maris would have two more shots at Fisher, in the fifth inning and the seventh. Both times he got under the ball and flied out to right, neither ball coming close to the fence. No. 61, if it was to come, would have to wait for another day.

When the game was over, Maris appeared on the *Red Barber Show* along with Mrs. Ruth, who seemed to have recovered from her disappointment. She had taken the attack on her husband's home run record as a personal affront, as if having the record broken would diminish the Babe's legend. When it began to look like Maris might break the record within the 154-game limit, Mrs. Ruth went to New Hampshire to escape baseball and news of the home run race.

Now, meeting Maris, Mrs. Ruth was gracious, and Roger, in turn, was humble, almost apologetic, about his accomplishment. He kissed her on the cheek and said, "I'm

Mrs. Claire Ruth, the Babe's widow, was at Yankee Stadium on September 26, 1961, to witness Roger Maris' 60th home run in the Yankees' 159th game that matched her husband's record for home runs in a season. After the game, Maris met with Mrs. Ruth, planted a kiss on her cheek and said, "I'm glad I didn't break Babe Ruth's record in 154 games. This record is enough for me." (AP IMAGES)

glad I didn't break Babe Ruth's record in 154 games. This record is enough for me."

Mrs. Ruth grabbed Roger's hand and said softly, "You had a great year. I want to congratulate you, and I mean that, Roger, sincerely. I know if the Babe were here, he would have wanted to congratulate you too."

Much later, when he reached his locker, there was a horde of reporters waiting to pepper him with more questions.

"What do you think about the commissioner's ruling now?"

"I have nothing to say about Mr. Frick," Maris replied. "He made the ruling. You talk to him about it. In a way, it's just as well I didn't break it [the record]. Don't ask me why. It's very hard to explain."

As he spoke, Maris fondled the ball that was hit for home run No. 60, now safely in his possession.

"I wanted this one, and I'm very glad I got it," he said. "I would like to get me one more. I don't care about the 59th anymore. I don't want it. This is the one I want now."

It was getting late. Maris had been answering reporters' questions for almost 20 minutes, and it was time to go.

"My wife is waiting," he said. "Do you think I can get out of here tonight?"

He removed his uniform and headed for the shower. He stopped abruptly and returned to his locker where he reached up, picked up the No. 60 baseball, and took it to the shower with him.

Chapter Twenty-Two

Gone Fishing

ON THE DAY AFTER HITTING HIS 60TH HOME RUN, the conquering hero arrived at Yankee Stadium and asked for the day off.

Looking at manager Ralph Houk's starting lineup and seeing that Hector Lopez was in right field batting second, Clete Boyer was at third base batting third, and Jack Reed was in center field batting seventh, reporters covering the Yankees were incredulous.

It was one thing to give up one at-bat by bunting with a runner on third and less than two outs and a game on the line as Roger Maris had done earlier in the season, but it was quite another to toss away four critical at-bats when you need just one home run to break the all-time single-season home run record and there were only four games left to do it.

"I'm going to give Roger a rest," Houk explained. "He's bushed."

Slowly, enterprising reporters began to piece together the series of events that caused such a bold move to evolve. For days, Maris had talked about being exhausted and needing a day off but said he would leave such a decision to his manager, who said he would let Maris play every game he wanted to play. But now, Maris didn't want to play.

Entering the Yankees' clubhouse on the morning of Wednesday, September 27, prior to a Ladies Day afternoon game against the Orioles, Maris marched directly into Houk's office.

Maris: "I'm beat, Skip. I need a day off."

Houk: "You can't take a day off; you're going for the record."

Maris: "I can't stand it anymore."

Houk: "Well, what should I tell the press when they see you're not here?"

Maris: "I don't know. Tell them I went fishing."

With the Orioles starting Steve Barber, a tough, hard-throwing left-hander, it was not a bad time to take a day off if you were going to take one. Although Maris never ducked any pitcher, he had not had much success hitting against Barber. In six at-bats in 1960, Maris had two hits, a single and a home run. But in 1961, he was hitless in 10 at-bats against him with four walks.

Maris left the stadium with his wife, and the two of them spent the afternoon shopping and then had a quiet dinner. With Maris and Mickey Mantle out of the lineup, the Yankees lost to the Orioles 3–2 Yogi Berra accounting for one run with his 22nd home run in the second, Hector Lopez driving in the second run with an RBI single in the eighth.

The Yankees were not scheduled the following day, which meant that Maris would have two consecutive days off. After sleeping late and having a leisurely hotel breakfast,

The day after he hit his 60th home run, Roger Maris took the day off and spent time catching up on his mail. (Photo by Charles Hoff/NY Daily News Archive via Getty Images)

the Marises spent the second day much like the first, shopping and then having a quiet, relaxing dinner.

The two days off worked wonders for Maris. He said he was the most relaxed he had been all year. When he returned to Yankee Stadium on September 29, he was refreshed and rejuvenated and ready for the Red Sox and the final three games of the season. He also arrived to discover that he was the eye of the storm in yet another controversy. Reporters were waiting for him, their inquiring minds wanting to know why he would take a day off and give up four at-bats when he was trying to break Babe Ruth's record.

"I can't win with you guys," Maris said. "You say I've played too many games to break the record. Then I don't play and you ask how I could miss a game when I'm going for the record."

With the American League pennant already safely put away and with the Boston Red Sox in town for the final three games of the season on September 29–October 1, it was not surprising that most of the talk around Yankee Stadium was about Maris and his chances of passing Ruth's home run record of 60.

Asked how he planned to attack Maris in the final three games, Red Sox manager Mike Higgins said, "We don't want to walk him. We want to give him a fair shot at the record, but we also want to get him out."

Among the Yankees' relief pitchers, the main topic of conversation was who among them would catch home run ball No. 61. They were planning to jockey for position in the bullpen to be best situated to catch a home run off Maris' bat.

A Sacramento restaurateur, Sam Gordon, had deposited in escrow a certified check for $5,000, which he would present to the fan who caught the 61st home run ball. Gordon would invite the fan and Maris to travel to Sacramento where Gordon would present the fan with the check and Maris with the ball while gaining more than $5,000 worth of publicity for his restaurant.

Yankees relief pitchers wondered why it had to be a fan that got the check. "Why not us?" they asked. Maris agreed. "As long as someone put up the offer, it should go for my teammates as well as anyone else," he said.

"I think I'll pick up a glove and go down there [to the bullpen] myself," joked manager Houk.

"I'm not even thinking about it [the money]," said Yankees' relief pitcher Hal Reniff. "I just think it would be a big thrill to say I caught the 61st homer. I'd be proud to present the ball to my teammate."

To open the series for the Red Sox, manager Higgins selected 14-game-winner Bill Monbouquette, who had beaten the Yankees 3–1 on a five-hitter five days earlier in Boston. In that game, he held Maris to a single in three official at-bats, walked him once, and retired him on fly balls to center and to left.

With a good percentage of the 21,485 fans clustered in the upper- and lower-right-field stands and the right-field bleachers, Maris failed to get the ball off the infield in four plate appearances against Monbouquette on this day.

In the first inning, Maris walked on a 3–2 pitch to a smattering of boos.

In the fourth inning, he hit a lazy pop fly to the shortstop.

In the sixth inning, he hit a foul pop to the first baseman.

In the ninth inning, with the score tied, 1–1, Maris again walked on a 3–2 pitch. The next batter, Roland Sheldon, who had entered to pitch in the eighth inning, bunted to first baseman Don Gile, who made a bad throw to second for an error, putting Yankees runners on first and second with none out. John Blanchard, who had accounted for the Yankees' first run with his 21st home run in the fourth, followed with a line single to right field that scored Maris with the winning run in a 2–1 victory for the Yankees.

"Monbouquette gave me good enough pitches, especially the last time, but I kept hitting under the ball and popping it up," said Maris. "I can't say he didn't give me enough chances, but I have no regrets."

The next afternoon drew a crowd of 29,182 that included more than 9,000 sandlot youngsters who were guests of the Yankees. The Red Sox pitcher was Don Schwall, a 15-game winner who would be voted American League Rookie of the Year in 1961. Schwall opposed the Yankees in Boston seven days earlier and gave up Mickey Mantle's 54th home run. He faced Maris four times, walking him twice. In his other at-bats, Maris reached on an error and grounded out.

Once again, Maris found Schwall's sinkerball perplexing and difficult to lift into the air. Maris drew a walk in the first inning and then hit three balls to the second baseman, Chuck Schilling, who scooped up the first two and threw Maris out at first. The third one scooted past Schilling into center field for a hit.

Schwall had started four games against the Yankees in his rookie season and he had held Maris to just three hits in 11 at-bats, all singles, walked him three times, and struck him out twice. Only once in 11 at-bats against Schwall was Maris able to lift the ball in the air.

More important, Maris had just one game left in which to hit the home run that would give him more home runs in a season than any other player in baseball history.

CHAPTER TWENTY-THREE

I Got You Babe!

EVER THE COUNTRY BOY, ROGER MARIS awakened early on the morning of Sunday, October 1, 1961. It was a cool but clear morning that would, by noon, morph into a beautiful, sun-splashed Indian summer day.

Maris' wife Pat, who had arrived from their Missouri home a few days earlier, also arose early. Roger ordered up a room service breakfast in their mid-Manhattan hotel, and then the couple strolled the few blocks to Fifth Avenue and 50th Street for the 8 AM Mass at St. Patrick's Cathedral.

Maris would walk Pat back to their hotel and then, as was his custom, he would leave Midtown and arrive at Yankee Stadium several hours before the scheduled 2 PM start of the final regular-season game of the year, against the Boston Red Sox. In her hotel, Pat Maris would await the arrival of their close friend, Julie Isaacson, who, accompanied by his wife, Selma, would drive to the stadium in plenty of time for the game's first pitch.

At the stadium, Maris went through what by now had become a familiar pregame ritual of pacing and smoking,

smoking and pacing. And he thought about what lay ahead of him. One more to go, he thought. Either he'd sink or swim, but he wouldn't go down without a fight.

"I figured I'd go down swinging," he said. "An 0–4 wouldn't hurt me now. I've done that before."

*

At approximately the same time Maris was arriving for work, Sal Durante, a 19-year-old, $60 per week truck driver and mechanic for an auto parts company and a rabid Yankees fan, was awakening at the modest home of his parents at 1418 Neptune Avenue in the Coney Island section of Brooklyn, 26.3 miles from Yankee Stadium.

"Nice day for a ballgame," Durante thought, so he telephoned his girlfriend, Rosemarie Calabrese, and told her to get ready. He was taking her to Yankee Stadium to see the Yankees play the Red Sox.

On the trip to Yankee Stadium, Durante mentioned that some guy in California was going to pay $5,000 to the person who caught the ball Maris hit for his 61st home run, and wouldn't it be nice if he caught the ball.

They arrived at the Stadium at 12:30 PM, an hour and a half before the first pitch. Normally, Durante would opt for the cheap seats (75¢ for bleachers or $1.30 for unreserved grandstand—even a $2.50 reserved seat was out of his price range), but this day was special. And Durante had a feeling. He had attended the Tuesday night game against Baltimore and had seats in Section 21 in right field, just inside fair territory.

Durante said he got to the park early that night and noticed during batting practice that "all the hitters, including Maris, seemed to hit the ball into Section 33."

So on Sunday, even though $3.50 per ticket was more than he had been accustomed to paying, Durante asked for, and received, two tickets in Section 33, seats 3 and 4 in box 163D, eight rows in back of the right-field wall and about 10' to the right of the bullpen.

*

It is difficult to understand, or explain, why on this day, with the prospect of being a witness to baseball history, the attendance was only 23,154 (or some 44,000 empty seats), or why Durante was able to get choice seats in right field just an hour and a half before game time.

Imagine the hysteria such an event would create today! Yankee Stadium would not be able to hold the number of people clamoring to attend a game of such magnitude, with a chance to see a player set a new single-season home run record. Souvenir hunters and get-rich-quick scammers would be jostling for position, hoping to be in the right place at the right time to catch the historic baseball. Auction houses Sotheby's, eBay, and Christie's would hope to broker the sale of the prized baseball that would bring upward of $1 million.

But in 1961, there was no such mania over possessing a mere $2.50 baseball. And no explanation for the stadium being two-thirds empty.

Some say the sparse crowd was because the pennant had already been clinched, rendering the game meaningless.

But a chance to witness the fall of Babe Ruth's single-season home run record could hardly be considered meaningless.

Others maintain that Yankees fans were still blasé enough not to be moved by one game or one event (in the '30s and '40s, it was said that "rooting for the Yankees is like rooting for U.S. Steel"), but in 1961, the Yankees would draw 1,747,725 patrons at home, their largest attendance in 10 years.

Although the memorabilia craze, so prevalent today, was not yet in full flower at the time, the offer of $5,000 by Sacramento restaurateur to the person who caught the 61st home run ball had been widely publicized and should have brought thousands of hopefuls to Yankee Stadium. Consider that in 1961, $5,000 was a princely sum that would cover the cost of two brand-new Dodge Lancers with enough money left over to purchase a year's supply of gasoline at a price of 31¢ per gallon.

The scheduled pitcher for the Red Sox was Tracy Stallard, a 24-year-old, hard-throwing rookie right-hander from Coeburn, Virginia.

"Maris didn't particularly concern me," Stallard told sportswriter Maury Allen in later years. "I had faced him a couple of times before and got him out." Actually, Stallard pitched against the Yankees three previous times in 1960 and 1961—one start and two relief appearances. He faced Maris four times and retired him all four times, on a strike-out, a pop-up to shortstop, a line drive to first, and a ground ball to second.

Pitching for the Yankees, Bill Stafford retired the Red Sox in order in the top of the first. In the bottom of the inning, Bobby Richardson hit a comebacker to Stallard and

Tony Kubek followed with a single to center. That brought up Maris. His appearance at the plate stirred the crowd.

Stallard fired a high, hard one that Maris took for ball one. The next pitch was a change-up that fooled Maris completely. He started his swing and was way out in front. His power was spent and the bat hit the ball with little force, sending a high, lazy pop fly to left field, an easy play for the Red Sox left fielder, Carl Yastrzemski.

In their next three at-bats, the Red Sox managed only one base runner, a leadoff single by catcher Russ Nixon in the third, while Stallard set the Yankees down in order in the second and third. The game was flying by. It was as if all the players, not just Maris, were nervous or that they were eager to see what Maris was going to do and didn't want to wait very long to find out.

In the bottom of the fourth, Kubek struck out and Maris came to bat for the second time. He waggled his 35", 33-ounce bat and then cocked it high behind his left ear as he looked out to the mound and eyed Stallard. Phil Rizzuto was at the microphone, describing the action on WCBS Radio, in New York. This was his call:

"Here comes Roger Maris. They're standing up, waiting to see if Roger is going to hit No. 61. Here's the windup... the pitch to Roger...way outside, ball one [boos]. *The fans are starting to boo...low, ball two...That one was in the dirt. And the boos get louder. Two balls, no strikes on Roger Maris. Here's the windup...fastball....HIT DEEP TO RIGHT... THIS COULD BE IT....HOLY COW! HE DID IT....61 HOME RUNS...They're fighting for the ball out there. Holy cow! Another standing ovation for Roger Maris."*

It was 2:43 on the huge stadium clock as the ball soared high and far toward Section 33 in the right-field stands and disappeared into a mass of humanity. What happened in Section 33 is open to debate.

Sal Durante: "When the ball was hit, I knew it was a homer. It was headed straight for me, but I thought it would land far behind me. Anyway, I stood up on my seat, put up my right hand, and the ball landed right in it."

Bud Daley, Yankees pitcher: "We [most of the Yankees' pitchers] had been in the bullpen for a couple of days, wearing our gloves and on our feet when Roger came up. When he finally did it, we scrambled all over the place to try and catch it, but the ball carried over our heads and into the seats."

Bob Turley, Yankees pitcher: "I was one of the guys in the bullpen, and the ball landed about 15' to my left and into the seats. There was a guy who had taken off his coat and was holding it above his head. The ball landed right in that coat, but there was a guy [Sal Durante] standing in the row behind him and he took the ball right out of the other guy's coat."

Bob Hale, Yankees first baseman/outfielder: "That's exactly what happened. Even though I was not a pitcher, I was in the bullpen because I spent a lot of time helping out as a bullpen catcher. I saw that kid [Durante] pick the ball right out of the other guy's coat."

Rosemarie Calabrese (Durante's girlfriend): "He [Durante] jumped up and said, 'I got it, I got it,' and before I knew just what he meant, the cops had him and were taking him away toward the Yankee bullpen."

The famed sweet and smooth left-handed batting stroke of Roger Maris as he connects against Tracy Stallard of the Boston Red Sox for home run No. 61 on October 1, 1961. (AP IMAGES)

When he connected with the pitch—solid, square, and powerful—Maris knew it was going out.

So did his teammates in the dugout, most of them clamoring to the top step when he came to bat.

So did the crowd. They reacted as one, letting out a mighty roar.

Maris paused momentarily at home plate to watch the ball sail into the seats, and then he lowered his head and began his triumphant journey around the bases. At first base, coach Wally Moses patted him on the back. As he approached third base, Frank Malzone, the Red Sox third baseman and a native of the Bronx, mouthed, "nice going." And when he reached third base, he was greeted by Frank Crosetti, the Yankees' third base coach.

As player and coach, Crosetti had been a Yankee for 30 years. He played with Babe Ruth, Lou Gehrig, and Joe DiMaggio. He helped groom Phil Rizzuto to be his replacement as Yankees shortstop. He coached Mickey Mantle, Yogi Berra, "Old Reliable" Tommy Henrich, and Charlie (King Kong) Keller. He had witnessed hundreds of home runs hit by dozens of Yankees, but only once had he shaken the hand of the Yankee who hit a home run as he rounded third, usually letting a slap on the back suffice. Not this time.

"If I had shaken the hand of everyone who hit a home run for the Yankees while I was the third base coach, I wouldn't have a hand left," he would say years later. "In my day, we didn't go in for all that handshaking and glamour stuff. But when Roger hit No. 61, I shook his hand. I slapped his back and then I followed him right down the third-base line, touching home plate right behind him. I felt like I had hit that home run, too."

At home plate, Yogi Berra, who had been on deck as the next hitter and had three bats slung over his shoulder, was waiting for Maris. Berra shook Maris' hand and patted him on the back as Maris jogged past him on his way to the dugout where his teammates were waiting with their own reception.

"I couldn't even think as I went around the bases," Maris said. "I was all fogged out. I was so happy I wasn't paying attention to anything that was going on. I just wanted to get around those bases and make it count."

In Lenox Hill hospital, Mickey Mantle, being treated for the abscess in his hip, sat on his bed and watched on television as Maris connected and became the man who hit more home runs in a season than any other player in baseball history.

"I got goose bumps," Mantle said.

The crowd was still on its feet, still clapping, still yelling his name as Maris ducked down into the Yankees' dugout. They continued to scream and clap and yell his name and they would not stop until Maris, the hero of this day, came out and acknowledged their greeting.

"He had to be pushed out of the dugout," remembered Bobby Richardson.

"Hector Lopez, Joe DeMaestri, and I pushed him out," Moose Skowron said.

"They kept pushing me out," Maris said. "They wouldn't let me sit down."

"I have a picture of the three of us pushing Roger on the field," said DeMaestri. "It's hanging in my office."

On the field, Maris, as he had done after hitting his 60th home run, waved his cap at the crowd and then disappeared back into the dugout.

When play resumed, Berra grounded out and John Blanchard popped out, two quick outs, and Maris picked up his glove and headed out to center field accompanied by more cheers and another standing ovation. As he passed second base, in a rare on-field gesture by a man in blue, second-base umpire Jim Honochick extended his hand, shook Maris' hand, and said, "Congratulations."

When the Yankees came to bat in the fifth inning, Maris was summoned to the clubhouse where Sal Durante was waiting with Yankees officials and security and holding the No. 61 home run ball.

"Congratulations," Maris said to Durante. "That's a good ball for you. You'll get a little money out of it."

Durante said he wasn't thinking about the money when he caught the ball—"Even if there's no reward, I'd give it to him," he said—but he wasn't going to turn down the $5,000 either. He would give some to his mother, and with the rest, he and Rosemarie could begin planning for their wedding.

When Maris came to bat in the sixth inning, he said to Red Sox catcher Russ Nixon, "Imagine that kid. He's planning to get married, but he'd give up the ball for nothing."

Maris said he was in no hurry for Durante to give him the ball.

"I want him to get what's coming to him," he said. "He's a real nice kid. I hope what he gets sets him off on his marriage. I wish him luck."

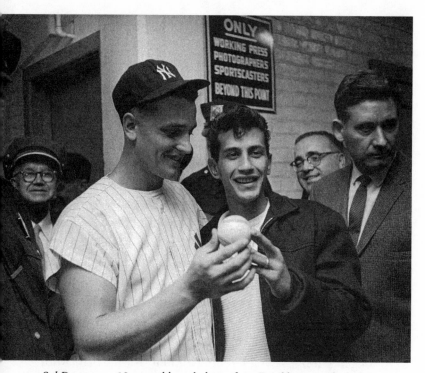

Sal Durante, a 19-year-old truck driver from Brooklyn, was the lucky young man who caught the baseball Roger Maris hit for his record 61st home run. Durante offered to give the ball to Maris, but the slugger refused, saying, "I want him to get what's coming to him." A Sacramento restaurateur paid Durante $5,000 for the ball. (AP IMAGES)

Maris struck out in the sixth. In the eighth, in his final at-bat of the game and the season, he popped to second, but his fourth-inning home run, No. 61, would hold up for the only run in a 1–0 victory, the Yankees' 109th of the season, the game played in a snappy 1:57.

When it was over and the clubhouse opened, a mob of reporters engulfed the area around Maris' locker. It was a scene that Yankees public relations director Bob Fishel would rue when he contemplated it in later years.

"If I only knew then what I know now," Fishel said. "The Roger Maris watch was the first of its kind in baseball history. We didn't have daily press conferences, because we had never been confronted with the problem before [a little more than a decade later, for example, when Pete Rose was chasing Joe DiMaggio's record of hitting in 56 consecutive games and Henry Aaron was zeroing in on Ruth's career record of 714 home runs, they held daily press conferences in stadiums using private rooms away from the clubhouse]. That would have been ideal for Roger because he could have gotten all the questions taken care of at once. But public relations was not nearly as advanced as it is today."

To the multitude assembled at his locker, Maris said, "Naturally, I'm glad to go past 60 even if I didn't do it in 154 [games]. I'd have liked to do it, but my season was longer. I'm not saying I'm up with him [Ruth]. Babe Ruth was a big man in baseball."

In what was for him a rare magnanimous gesture, Maris acknowledged and paid tribute to the stadium crowd and to Stallard, the Red Sox pitcher.

"I don't think there's anything a player wants more than to have the people with him," he said.

Of Stallard, Maris said, "He's just a rookie, but I appreciate the guy was man enough to pitch to me. He tried to get me out, and I tried to hit it out."

In the Red Sox's clubhouse, Stallard was asked how it felt to be linked with Tom Zachary, the Washington Senators pitcher who gave up Ruth's 60th home run exactly 34 years and one day earlier.

"I don't feel badly at all," Stallard said. "Why should I? The guy got a bunch of other pitchers for 60 homers before he got to me. I started against him three times, and this was the only homer he hit off me. Look, I was just trying to get him out like everyone else. I got behind two balls in the count and I didn't want to walk him. I came in with a fastball, and that was it. I'm not going to lose any sleep over this. I'd rather have given up the home run than to have walked him."

Finally, Maris said, "No one knows how tired I am. I'm happy I got past 60, but I'm so tired. I'm just glad it's over."

It was over. He had hit more home runs in a season than any other player, more than his teammate and friend, Mickey Mantle; more than Hank Greenberg and Jimmie Foxx; and more than the man himself, Babe Ruth. With or without an asterisk, Roger Maris stood alone.

Epilogue I

THREE DAYS AFTER THE EUPHORIA of Roger Maris' 61st home run, the Yankees hosted the Cincinnati Reds at Yankee Stadium in the first game of baseball's 58th World Series. The Yankees took the Series opener 2–0 behind the brilliant two-hit, complete game pitching of Whitey Ford, who was staging his own pursuit of Babe Ruth—the record for consecutive scoreless innings by a pitcher in the World Series.

In the World Series of 1916 and 1918, Ruth, then in his early twenties and pitching for the Boston Red Sox, had hurled 29⅔ consecutive scoreless innings. With shutouts of the Pittsburgh Pirates in Games 3 and 6 of the 1960 World Series and this one against Cincinnati, Ford had pitched 27 consecutive scoreless World Series innings. He would break the record in the third inning of Game 4 and then, noting Maris' 61 home runs and his own scoreless streak, he would crack, "Poor Babe. He's having a bad year."

In pitching his third consecutive World Series shutout, Ford was aided by two spectacular defensive plays by third baseman Clete Boyer and supported offensively by solo home runs from Elston Howard in the fourth inning and Moose Skowron in the sixth.

Perhaps in an emotional hangover, Maris was hitless in four at-bats with one strikeout. Mickey Mantle, still in excruciating pain from the abscess in his right hip that by now was a gaping hole oozing a mixture of pus and blood, did not play.

The Reds answered back to win Game 2, behind the pitching of Joey Jay, the hitting of Gordy Coleman (two-run homer) and Johnny Edwards (RBI single, RBI double), and the derring-do on the base paths of Elio Chacon, who scored from third in the fifth inning on a short passed ball with what proved to be the winning run.

Again, Maris was hitless (he walked once and struck out twice), and Mantle did not play.

Having tied the Series at a game apiece, the Reds' confidence was boosted since they would be returning home to the friendly confines of Crosley Field for the next three games.

Mantle returned to the lineup in Game 3 but was hitless in four at-bats, two strikeouts and two fly balls to center field. Bill Stafford for the Yankees and 16-game-winning knuckle-baller Bob Purkey for the Reds battled superbly through the first six innings, the Reds producing the only run in the third inning on an RBI double by Frank Robinson.

The Yankees tied the score in the top of the seventh when Yogi Berra blooped a single to right to score Tony Kubek, who had singled and moved to second on a passed ball. But the Reds regained the lead in the bottom of the seventh when Johnny Edwards doubled and scored on a single by Eddie Kasko that knocked Stafford out of the game.

With Purkey and the Reds needing just four outs for a win and a 2–1 lead in the Series, John Blanchard, who had specialized in pinch-hit home runs during the season, did it again. He stunned the Cincinnati crowd by belting a game-tying, pinch-hit, two-out home run off Purkey in the eighth inning. Roger Maris led off the top of the ninth for the Yankees and finally awoke from his reverie, driving a Purkey slider deep into the right-field seats to put the Yankees ahead, 3–2. It would be Maris' only home run of the Series.

Luis Arroyo, who entered the game in the eighth, stranded a runner on second in the bottom of the ninth, and the Yankees nailed down the victory to go ahead in the Series 2–1.

In Game 4, Maris was hitless in three at-bats but walked twice and scored two runs. Mantle got his only hit of the Series, a single in the fourth. Then, with blood from the abscess in his right hip seeping through his uniform pants leg, he was removed for a pinch runner (Elston Howard would later say that when he went to the trainer's room to check on Mantle and he saw the ugly, gaping wound in his teammate's leg, it brought tears to the catcher's eyes).

Hector Lopez ran for Mantle and then went to right field in the bottom of the fourth with Maris moving to center.

Ford held the Reds scoreless through the fifth to break Ruth's record for consecutive scoreless World Series innings by a pitcher but left leading 2–0 because of an ankle injury. Jim Coates came in to hold the Reds to one hit over the last four innings. Meanwhile, with Lopez, Skowron, and Boyer picking up the slack on offense, the Yankees scored two runs in the sixth and three more in the seventh for a 7–0 victory and were now up in the Series 3–1.

In Game 5, the Yankees scored five runs in the top of the first and blew the Reds away 13–5 to capture the 19th

World Series championship in their history. Playing in place of Mantle and Yogi Berra (stiff shoulder), Hector Lopez and Johnny Blanchard each homered and between them collected five hits and drove in seven runs.

With Mantle playing in only two of the five games (he had one hit in six at-bats) and Maris getting only two hits in 19 at-bats, a .105 average, it was a testament to the depth of the Yankees that they should make short work of the National League champions. Blanchard led them in home runs with two and in batting average with .400; Lopez led in RBIs with seven. Bobby Richardson batted .391, Moose Skowron .353, and Lopez .333.

*

A half century later, there are many who proclaim the 1961 Yankees baseball's greatest team, while old timers—many of the same people who rued the thought of Roger Maris breaking Babe Ruth's single-season home run record—held out for the '27 Yankees of Ruth, Lou Gehrig, Tony Lazzeri, Waite Hoyt, and Herb Pennock as baseball's greatest team.

The '61 Yankees won 109 of 162 games, a winning percentage of .673; finished eight games ahead in the American League; and won the World Series 4–1 over Cincinnati.

The '27 Yankees won 110 of 154 games, a winning percentage of .714 (curiously the exact number of career home runs hit by Ruth); finished 19 games ahead in the American League; and won the World Series 4–0 over Pittsburgh.

The '61 Yankees led the 10-team American League in home runs (a major league record 240), slugging percentage (.442), fielding percentage (.980), and double plays (180).

The '27 Yankees led the eight-team American League in home runs (158), hits (1,644), runs (976), batting average (.307), on-base percentage (.384), slugging percentage (.488), walks (642), triples (103), earned run average (3.20), and shutouts (11).

The game had changed markedly in the 34 years that separated the 1927 and 1961 Yankees, the most glaring changes being the proliferation of home runs and the emergence of the relief pitcher to the detriment of the starting pitcher. Although the 1961 Yankees hit 82 more home runs than the 1927 Yankees (240–158), the disparity between the two teams is strictly a sign of the times.

In 1927, Ruth and Gehrig hit 107 home runs. In 1961, Maris and Mantle hit 115. In 1927, Tony Lazzeri was third on the Yankees in home runs with 18, and no other Yankee hit more than 8. In 1961, three Yankees catchers, Yogi Berra (22), Elston Howard (21), and John Blanchard (21) combined for 64 homers, and seven Yankees (Maris, Mantle, Moose Skowron, Berra, Howard, Blanchard, and Clete Boyer) produced double figures in homers.

"When I think of the 1961 season, I think about all the home runs," said Bobby Richardson. "And I think about the starting lineup and the fact that, with no DH, we had three catchers with more than 60 home runs. And then I think of the fact that the starting infield had sweatshirts made up after the season and printed on the shirts was the number of home runs we each hit and I was embarrassed to wear it because I hit only three."

But the 1961 Yankees hit only 51 more home runs than the league runner-up, the Los Angeles Angels, while the '27 Yankees hit 102 more home runs than the league runner-up, the Philadelphia Athletics. In 1927, Ruth alone hit more home runs than 13 major league teams.

When Ralph Houk took over from Casey Stengel as manager of the Yankees in 1961, his first major decision was to install a four-man starting rotation (Stengel had a five-man rotation). The impetus for the move was to give the team's ace, Whitey Ford, more starting opportunities. It resulted in Ford's finest year and his only Cy Young Award.

Prior to 1961, Ford's best year was 1956 when he was 19–6 with a league-leading 2.47 earned run average. That year he made 30 starts, completed 18 of them, pitched 225⅔ innings, and struck out 141.

In 1961, he won 25 games, a career high, lost only four, and had career highs in starts with 39, innings pitched with 283, and strikeouts with 209. Although his complete games dropped to 11, that was due largely to the emergence of Luis Arroyo, who won 15 games in relief and led the American League with 29 saves.

The Yankees of '61 had six pitchers with double figures in wins—Ford, Arroyo, Bill Stafford, Ralph Terry, Roland Sheldon, and Jim Coates—but only 47 complete games, fourth-most in the American League.

The '27 Yankees were second in the league in complete games with 82 and also had six pitchers with double figures in wins—Waite Hoyt with 22; Herb Pennock, 19; Wilcey Moore, 19; Urban Shocker, 18; Dutch Ruether, 13; and George Pipgras, 10.

Moore was the '27 Yankees' top reliever. He appeared in 50 games, made 12 starts, pitched 213 innings, and saved 13 games in addition to his 19 wins (saves were not recorded at the time, but in perusing box scores years later, statisticians determined the number of saves that would have been recorded). In 1961, Arroyo appeared in 65 games, all in relief, pitched 119 innings, and won 15 games to go with his 29 saves.

In their four-game sweep of the Pirates in the World Series, the '27 Yankees used only four pitchers (Hoyt, Moore, Pennock, and Pipgras) and got complete-game victories from Moore, Pennock, and Pipgras.

The '61 Yankees used six pitchers in their five-game World Series triumph of Cincinnati and had only one complete game.

One area in which there is no debate over which team was superior is defense, especially in the infield. It's not even a contest. The '61 Yankees' infield of Moose Skowron, Bobby Richardson, Tony Kubek, and Clete Boyer has the nod over the '27 infield of Lou Gehrig, Tony Lazzeri, Mark Koenig, and Joe Dugan. The '61 Yankees led the American League in fielding percentage at .980 (the '27 Yankees fielded .969), in double plays with 180 (123 for the '27 team), and in fewest errors with 124 (to 196 for the 1927 Yankees).

Epilogue II

Roger Maris had broken baseball's most cherished record; indeed, the most celebrated record in all of sports. He was the all-time single-season home run king. His team had won the World Series. He was named the winner of the prestigious Hickok Belt, valued at $10,000 and awarded to the year's outstanding professional athlete. For the second straight year, he had been voted the American League's Most Valuable Player in another close vote with his teammate Mickey Mantle (Maris won by a mere four votes and had seven first-place votes to Mantle's six). And he was planning to move his large family into a bigger house in Independence, Mo., not far from the home of former President Harry S. Truman.

In 1962, Maris should have been sitting on top of the world, amassing untold riches, receiving a healthy raise from the Yankees over his 1961 contract, and basking in the adulation of fans and the admiration of his peers.

He wasn't.

It was, in fact, in 1962, when Maris should have been at the height of his career and his popularity that things turned sour for him.

Yes, there was money to be made—a barnstorming home run exhibition tour with other sluggers Rocky Colavito, Jim

Gentile, and Harmon Killebrew; speaking engagements; television appearances; a movie, *Safe At Home*, in which Maris and Mantle played themselves and arranged cameo roles for their friend Julie Isaacson and their friend and teammate Whitey Ford. From his historic, record-breaking achievement, Maris accrued an estimated $150,000 total from all income over and above his Yankees salary. Although it was a munificent amount for the time, it was a mere pittance by today's standards and hardly what one might have expected his magnificent feat to be worth.

There had been an incident during the winter when Maris abruptly left a banquet in Milwaukee to make a plane flight to fulfill a previous commitment in another city. In so doing, Maris was forced to brush past several youngsters waiting for his autograph. When word of his actions reached members of the media, Roger was vilified in print and in commentary on radio and television.

In addition, there was an acrimonious salary negotiation with the Yankees on his 1962 contract (there were no long-term contracts for baseball players in those days, no arbitration, no free agency, and no agents).

When he was traded to the Yankees in 1960, Maris was earning a salary of $19,000. After hitting 39 home runs, leading the American League with 112 RBIs, and being named Most Valuable Player, the Yankees rewarded him by bumping his salary up to $37,500, a raise of almost 100 percent.

Now he was armed with even stronger arguments, the single-season home run record, a tie for the league lead in RBIs with 141, a second straight MVP award, a World Series title, and having helped put people in the seats at Yankee

Stadium (the Yankees' 1961 attendance of 1,747,725 was their highest in 10 years and an increase of 120,376 customers over the previous season). One interesting note on Maris' 1961 RBI total: At first, Maris was awarded the RBI title with 142, one more than Jim Gentile of the Baltimore Orioles and two more than the Tigers' Rocky Colavito. Thirty-four years later, members of SABR, the Society of Baseball Researchers, in going over old score sheets, discovered an error in the recordkeeping that awarded Maris an RBI he hadn't earned. In 2010, the correction was officially entered into the record. Maris and Gentile tied for the 1961 American League lead in RBIs with 141, one more than Colavito. However, at the same time, it was discovered that Maris had also been deprived of a run scored. That, too, was added to the official records, giving Maris 131 runs and the AL lead by one over teammate Mickey Mantle.

Although he acknowledged he did not expect to earn what Mantle was making (Mickey had recently signed his contract calling for $82,000), Maris figured with perfect logic that his 1961 season should be worth at least a 100 percent raise, boosting his salary to $75,000.

Ralph Kiner, a seven-time National League home run champion for the Pittsburgh Pirates in the 1940s and '50s was famously quoted as saying, "Home run hitters drive Cadillacs," and, indeed, home run hitters have long been among the game's highest-paid players. Babe Ruth was earning $10,000 from the Boston Red Sox in 1919, but after joining the Yankees and hitting 54 and 59 home runs in back-to-back seasons, his salary jumped to $52,000. By 1930, he was earning $80,000, a veritable king's ransom at the time. When told he was making more money than the

President of the United States, Herbert Hoover, the Babe replied, "I had a better year than Hoover."

Maris believed his time had come to cash in on his record-breaking season, but when he received his contract, it called for $50,000—a raise of $12,500, or a mere 33 percent increase.

Maris was disappointed. He was hurt. He was insulted. And he was angry.

He returned the contract unsigned, setting off a series of back and forth negotiations that lasted several weeks. The Yankees upped their offer to $60,000 and then to $65,000, but Maris would not cave in. He remained adamant and stubborn.

With the start of spring training only days away, Maris decided to drive to Florida without a contract, figuring he could work out a deal in a face-to-face meeting with general manager Roy Hamey. Soon after arriving in Fort Lauderdale, the Yankees' new spring-training home, Maris met with Hamey and the two men reached a compromise. Maris would earn $72,500 in 1962, $9,500 less than Mantle and a raise of $35,000. Not quite the 100 percent raise Maris was seeking but close enough.

When word of the contract dispute was leaked to the press, Maris did not come across as a shrewd negotiator fighting for what he believed was his due and to provide for his growing family. Instead, he was portrayed by the media as a typically spoiled and coddled professional athlete and was blasted for his ingratitude and greed.

As spring training 1962 was getting underway, the city fathers of Fort Lauderdale held a gala brunch as a way of welcoming the Yankees to their community. It was a command performance for all members of the team and its executives with a place of honor on the dais reserved for their biggest stars, the M&M Boys, sitting alongside one another. Among those in attendance were community leaders, some of whom brought along their children.

During a lull in the proceedings, a young boy approached Maris, handed him a pen and paper, and politely requested an autograph. Maris took the pen and paper, turned to Mantle and said, "Watch this," and scrawled a large "X" on the paper and handed it back to the boy.

It was not done out of malice, Maris would later explain. It was meant as a good-natured and playful tease. His plan, Maris said, was to watch the disappointed look on the boy's face and then ask for the paper back and provide the youngster with his bona-fide autograph. The plan went awry, however, when the boy grabbed the paper without looking at what was written on it and beat a hasty retreat with his souvenir, vanishing in the crowd.

The boy returned to his seat and showed the piece of paper to his father, who was so irate he later telephoned the sports department of the local newspaper to complain about the boorish and antisocial behavior of that misanthrope, Maris.

The story, unflattering as it was, hit the paper the next day, was picked up by the wire services, and was sent around the country, setting off a firestorm of controversy and anti-Maris reaction. Among those eager to take Maris to task were two of the most powerful sportswriters in the land, Oscar Fraley, columnist for United Press International who also was the author of the best-selling book and eventual television series, *The Untouchables*, and Jimmy Cannon of

"Nobody Asked Me But..." fame, the sports columnist for the *New York Journal-American* whose column was widely syndicated across the country and, consequently, reached millions.

"If either of my sons has a hero, I hope it's John Glenn," wrote Fraley, who was never anywhere near Fort Lauderdale that spring. "Guys like Roger Maris bat a round zero with me."

Cannon, a lifetime bachelor and New York City resident with ties to influential people in town, had formed a relationship with Maris in the player's two seasons with the Yankees. They seemed to enjoy one another's company, occasionally breakfasting together in Manhattan. But when Cannon tried to talk with Maris the day after the Fort Lauderdale flak, Roger said, "I'm not talking to anyone, and that includes you."

Cannon wrote two especially vicious columns about Maris, one that was titled "Maris the Whiner," and a second in which he wrote that Maris envied Mantle and that the two sluggers were feuding and their strained relationship was destroying the morale of the team.

Other writers joined the fray and jumped on the anti-Maris bandwagon. In the *Miami News,* columnist Tommy Devine wrote, "If it weren't for sportswriters, Roger Maris probably would be an $18-a-week clerk at the A&P back in Missouri."

Maris reacted predictably, declaring he no longer would speak with writers, which only served to exacerbate the situation.

Chastised almost daily by some sportswriter, Maris was growing more irritable by the day as spring training was winding down. On Thursday, March 22, the Yankees were scheduled to play an exhibition game in Al Lang Field in St. Petersburg, their former longtime training base. Their opponents would be the new kid on the block in New York baseball, the expansion New York Mets, managed by the Yankees' former manager, Casey Stengel. It would be the historic first meeting between the Yankees and the fledgling Mets.

Before the game, an enterprising photographer got the idea of posing Maris with the Mets' hitting instructor, Rogers Hornsby—a Hall of Famer, the National League's all-time leading hitter with a career batting average of .358, and one of the most ornery of men.

Joe DeMaestri had played for Hornsby in 1952 when Hornsby managed the St. Louis Browns. According to DeMaestri, Hornsby was so disliked by his players that many on the team were ready to go on strike and refuse to play for him. When Browns owner Bill Veeck learned of the possible insurrection, he joined the team in Boston, fired Hornsby, and replaced him with the Browns' respected and well-liked veteran shortstop, Marty Marion.

"We all chipped in and gave Veeck a huge trophy for liberating us," said DeMaestri.

Hornsby had not mellowed in the intervening years when, in the spring of 1962, a photographer asked him to pose with Maris. What the photographer either didn't know or failed to consider is that Hornsby had been among the most outspoken against Maris during the home run race, stating that Maris was unworthy of breaking a record held by the great Babe Ruth.

The photographer approached Hornsby, sitting in the Mets' dugout, and asked if he would pose for a picture with Roger Maris.

"Yeah, I'll pose with him," Hornsby said. "Bring him over."

With that, Hornsby got off the bench, left the Mets' dugout, and headed for the batting cage where he expected to be joined by Maris. Meanwhile the photographer approached Maris in the Yankees' dugout and asked him if he would pose with Hornsby.

Obviously still fuming about being bad-mouthed by Hornsby the previous season, Maris turned his back on the photographer and walked away without saying a word. Observing this display, Hornsby angrily left the batting cage and returned to the dugout, where he was met by a gathering of writers who had witnessed the snub by Maris and wanted Hornsby's explanation of what had happened.

"He's a busher," Hornsby growled. "He couldn't carry my bat. He's a little punk ballplayer."

*

Most players would consider 33 home runs and 100 RBIs a huge, breakout year. To Roger Maris and Yankees fans, those numbers accumulated by Maris in the 1962 season were a major disappointment.

He had entered the 1962 season as the all-time single-season home run leader, the defending American League home run and RBI champion, and a two-time defending American League Most Valuable Player. Expectations were high. Fans expected (demanded?) more from Maris. They went to games hoping, even expecting, to see him hit a home run. When he didn't, they were gravely disappointed.

Maris' 33 home runs represented a drop of 28 from the previous year. Harmon Killebrew, Norm Cash, Rocky Colavito, and Leon (Daddy Wags) Wagner hit more. Jim Gentile hit as many. Maris' 100 RBIs were 41 fewer than the year before. Killebrew, Norm Siebern, Colavito, Floyd Robinson, Wagner, Lee Thomas, and Bob Allison all had more. Hobbled by injuries, Mickey Mantle appeared in only 123 games, hit 30 home runs, and drove in 89 runs—thereby, in large measure, effectively depriving Maris of the protection in the Yankees' lineup he had enjoyed in his record season.

Nevertheless, Maris helped the Yankees win a second consecutive pennant and World Series, over the San Francisco Giants in seven games. Although he failed to hit well in the Series (a .174 average, one home run, five RBIs), Maris showed his versatility and his defensive prowess with a game-saving play in the ninth inning of the decisive seventh game.

It came with the Yankees leading 1–0 with two outs and Matty Alou on first base. Willie Mays ripped a scorching line drive into right field. When it left the bat, the ball appeared headed for the corner, probably all the way to the wall, where it would rattle around and allow Alou to score easily with the tying run and Mays to carry the winning run to third base. But Maris, reacting instinctively and quickly, cut the ball off, whirled, and fired a strike to second baseman Bobby Richardson, holding Alou on third. When Willie McCovey followed with a screaming line drive into Richardson's glove, the game was over and the Yankees had won their 20th World Series.

*

After the 1962 season, Maris would hit only 70 more home runs and drive in 194 runs in four more years as a Yankee. In 1963, reduced to 90 games by a series of injuries, Maris' home runs fell off to 23, his RBIs to 53. Relatively injury-free in 1964, he hit 26 homers and drove in 71 runs, but the numbers don't tell the full story. On August 22, the Yankees were five-and-a-half games out of first place and Mickey Mantle was again hobbled with injuries, his ability to play center field drastically curtailed. Maris took over the position and practically carried the Yankees across the finish line. He batted .304, hit seven homers, and drove in 24 runs as the Yankees won 30 of their final 41 games and captured the American League pennant by one game over the Chicago White Sox.

After winning four consecutive American League pennants and two World Series, the Yankees, afflicted with aging stars, floundered in 1965, and so did Maris. The Yanks would win only 77 games and finish in sixth place, their poorest season in 40 years. Maris' woes were mostly physical. He played in only 46 games, hit eight home runs, drove in 27 runs, and batted .239.

One day in June, Maris slid into home plate and injured his right hand. He was in such pain that he could not play the next day. The Yankees sent him for X-rays, which showed no structural damage, but the pain persisted. The Yankees kept reporting that Maris' return to the lineup was "day to day," and Maris kept insisting that he was in pain. As a result, there were rumors circulating that the injury, and the pain, was not in Maris' hand but in his head. He was unfairly branded a malingerer.

When the pain persisted and was so bad that he could hardly stand it, Maris felt he had no choice, considering the Yankees' attitude, but to seek a second opinion. New X-rays showed a broken bone lodged in the upper right side of the hand and Maris, without the Yankees' knowledge, scheduled an operation in the final days of the season.

When the Yankees learned of the operation, they were livid.

In 1966, the Yankees sank further in the standings, finishing in last place for the first time since 1912, when the American League was an eight-team league. Maris, 31 years old and damaged goods, was reduced to a part-time player as the Yankees tried to infuse the team with young players such as Joe Pepitone, Tom Tresh, Bobby Murcer, and Roy White.

Maris batted .233 with 13 home runs and 43 RBIs. Clearly, he was no longer the home run and RBI threat he had been just a few years earlier. More important, he no longer had the competitive desire that had driven him to success. He told manager Ralph Houk that he was planning to retire and not return in 1967.

That winter, the Yankees traded Maris to the St. Louis Cardinals for Charley Smith, a journeyman third baseman who would bat .239, hit 69 home runs, and drive in 281 in 10 major league seasons playing for seven different teams.

Because St. Louis was only a 250-mile drive on I-70 from his home in Independence, and because the Cardinals had the nucleus of a contending team, Maris agreed to postpone his retirement and play one season in St. Louis. He fit seamlessly as the right fielder on a team that had Orlando Cepeda at first base, Julian Javier at second, Dal Maxvill at shortstop, Mike Shannon (who agreed to move from right field to accommodate Maris) at third, Lou Brock in left field, Curt Flood in center, Tim McCarver catching, and a pitching staff headed by Bob Gibson, Steve Carlton, and Nelson Briles.

Although no longer the home run threat of his earlier years, Maris was a great addition to the Cardinals, a veteran player with big-game experience, a productive player, and a much beloved teammate. In 125 games, he batted .261, hit nine home runs, drove in 55 runs, and was a vital contributor to a championship team. In the World Series against the Boston Red Sox, won by the Cardinals in seven games, he batted .385, hit a home run, and drove in seven runs. He drove in both of the Cardinals' runs in their 2–1 victory in Game 1. In Game 4, he doubled home the first two runs in a 6–0 victory. And in Game 5, his ninth-inning homer was the Cardinals' only run in a 3–1 defeat.

Once again, Maris talked about retiring to spend more time with his growing family, but when he mentioned his plans to Cards owner, beer magnate Gussie Busch, Maris was made an offer he couldn't refuse. Maris had long talked of owning a beer distributorship when he was no longer playing baseball, and here was his opportunity knocking. Play one more season, Busch said, and he would arrange for Maris to acquire a Budweiser distributorship. It was an enticing offer for a man eager to provide for his family.

Maris played his final season in 1968. Although he was used sparingly and appeared in only 100 games, he helped the Cardinals win their second straight pennant by batting .255 with five home runs and 45 RBIs (in 12 major league seasons, Maris played on teams that won seven pennants and three World Series). But in the World Series of 1968, he would get only three hits and drive in one run in 19 at-bats.

*

Now Roger Maris knew for certain that it was time to hang up his glove and get on with the rest of his life.

True to his word, Gussie Busch awarded Maris a Budweiser distributorship. Although he was reluctant to leave his home in Independence, Mo., the only available Budweiser distributorship was in Gainesville, Florida, and Maris knew this was too enticing an opportunity to pass up. He moved his family to Gainesville, where he lived the life of a country squire and entrepreneur while never losing his simplicity. He even coached a local high school baseball team, Oak Hill High, which named its field after him.

In 1983, Maris was diagnosed with Hodgkin's lymphoma. For years, so hurt was he over his treatment by the Yankees, he remained estranged from the team, refusing to return to Yankee Stadium for Old Timers' Day. It was Yankees owner George M. Steinbrenner who brought about reconciliation with Maris, reaching out to him and convincing him that his rancor was with a previous Yankees administration. Maris agreed to return to Yankee Stadium for Old Timers' Day on July 21, 1984, but for the most part kept the serious nature of his illness a secret.

A crowd of 33,435—many of whom were probably among those who booed him two decades before—accorded Maris a rousing, welcoming, standing ovation as the Yankees announced that his No. 9 would be permanently retired and a plaque honoring him would be dedicated and hung in Monument Park at the stadium. The plaque reads:

ROGER EUGENE MARIS
AGAINST ALL ODDS
IN 1961 HE BECAME THE ONLY PLAYER TO HIT
MORE THAN 60 HOME RUNS IN A SINGLE SEASON
IN BELATED RECOGNITION OF ONE OF BASEBALL'S
GREATEST ACHIEVEMENTS EVER
HIS 61 IN '61
THE YANKEES SALUTE HIM AS A GREAT PLAYER
AND AS AUTHOR OF ONE OF THE MOST
REMARKABLE CHAPTERS IN THE HISTORY
OF MAJOR LEAGUE BASEBALL

"When I saw Roger on Old Timers' Day," said Moose Skowron, "I noticed something in his mouth, and I said, 'Roger, did you get new teeth?' He didn't say anything to me, but a year later, I went to the Roger Maris Golf Tournament in Fargo, North Dakota, and a doctor friend of Roger said to me, 'You know, Moose, you're the only one who asked a question about his teeth.' I didn't know anything. I just happened to notice that there was something wrong with his teeth. I don't know if they had been pulled or if they gave him new ones, but there was something different and it turned out it was because of the cancer."

Roger Maris died on December 14, 1985, in M.D. Anderson Hospital in Houston, Texas. His body was shipped to Fargo, the town where he spent his teenage years, first attracted attention as an athlete, and which he always

Two decades after their celebrated home run chase, Roger Maris (left) and Mickey Mantle, both retired, get together before a game at Yankee Stadium. (PHOTO BY FOCUS ON SPORT/GETTY IMAGES)

considered his home. His funeral Mass was said in Fargo's St. Mary's Cathedral. His Yankees teammates Mickey Mantle, Whitey Ford, Clete Boyer, and Moose Skowron, all members of the 1961 team, served as pallbearers. Another teammate from the '61 team, Bobby Richardson, delivered the eulogy. Maris was buried in Fargo's Holy Cross Cemetery. He was three months and four days past his 51st birthday.

In Fargo, there is a Roger Maris Drive, a Roger Maris Museum, and The Roger Maris Cancer Center.

*

"*He didn't have overwhelming career statistics, but in 1961 he did something that has never been done by anyone else before or since: he got 61 home runs in a single season. Somewhere along the line, they are going to have to recognize the fact that he hit those 61 home runs and that he did it playing alongside one of the greatest players of all-time—Mister Mantle. I would be inclined to think that Maris deserves to be in the Hall of Fame.*"

—Ted Williams, writing in his book *Ted Williams' Hit List*, published by Stoddart Publishing Co. in 1995

Roger Maris is "*a Hall of Famer for sure in my book.*"
—Mickey Mantle, writing in his book *My Favorite Summer 1956,* published by Doubleday in 1991

Maris' name appeared on the ballot for 15 years. In the first 11 years of his eligibility, his highest placing was 10th, in 1984, and the highest percentage of votes he received was

29.4 in 1979. In 1985, after it was learned that he had been diagnosed with Hodgkin's lymphoma, he jumped from 10th on the ballot to 7th and from 26.6 percent of the vote to 32.4 percent. The following year, after his death, he was fifth on the ballot with 41.6 percent. In 1988, his final year of eligibility through the vote of the BBWAA, Maris was fifth on the ballot with his highest percentage, 43.1.

In his years on the ballot, Maris polled more votes than Hal Newhouser once, Richie Ashburn twice, Luis Aparicio twice, Orlando Cepeda six times, and Bill Mazeroski eight times, all of whom were elected to the Baseball Hall of Fame.

After his eligibility through vote of the baseball writers had passed, Maris became the purview of the Veterans Committee, comprised of all living members of the Hall of Fame. Before being placed on the ballot to be judged by the Veterans Committee, eligible players must be passed on by a screening committee that reduces the final ballot to 10 names. Members of the Veterans Committee can vote on up to four players and, as with the BBWAA vote, a player must receive the requisite 75 percent of the votes cast. The Veterans Committee votes every two years.

Maris' name first appeared on the Veterans Committee ballot in 2003. Eighty-one votes were cast, with 61 votes needed for election. Maris received 18 votes, or 22.2 percent. In 2005, 80 votes were cast. Maris received 19 votes, or 23.7 percent, 41 votes short of election. In 2007, he received 15 of the 82 votes cast, 47 short of election. His name was not included on the 2009 Veterans Committee ballot, a strong indication that Maris' chances of being elected the Hall of Fame have come and gone.

Although Roger Maris has not been enshrined in the Baseball Hall of Fame, he has not been forgotten in Cooperstown, nor has he been ignored. On display in the museum is the bat Maris used to hit his 61st home run and the ball he hit. It was caught by Sal Durante, who sold it for $5,000 to Sacramento restaurateur Sam Gordon, who returned the ball to Maris after putting it on display for several years. The ball was donated to the Hall of Fame by the Maris family in 1973.

Epilogue III

Babe Ruth's record of 60 home runs in a single season had lasted 33 years when Roger Maris broke it in 1961.

Maris held the record 37 years until Mark McGwire broke it with 70 home runs in 1998.

McGwire held the record for three years until Barry Bonds broke it with 73 home runs in 2001.

In a four-year span, from 1998–2001, Maris' record of 61 home runs in a season was surpassed six times by three players.

- Sammy Sosa—66 in 1998, 63 in 1999, 64 in 2001
- Mark McGwire—70 in 1998, 65 in 1999
- Barry Bonds—73 in 2001

Sosa, McGwire, and Bonds all have been mentioned in connection with baseball's apparently rampant steroids scandal, their home run totals therefore tainted, shrouded in doubt, and open to serious question. Roger Maris has never been accused of, or thought to have, circumvented the rules in any manner. He therefore reigns as the last of the "pure" home run record holders, an accomplishment that baseball might want to consider denoting with a "distinctive mark."

You mean with an asterisk?

Sources

Books

Allen, Maury. *Roger Maris: A Man for All Seasons*. New York: Donald I. Fine, Inc., 1986.

Creamer, Robert W. *Stengel: His Life and Times*. New York: Simon & Schuster, 1984.

Ford, Whitey, with Phil Pepe. *Slick: My Life in and Around Baseball*. New York: William Morrow & Co., 1987.

Ford, Whitey, with Phil Pepe. *Few and Chosen: Defining Yankee Greatness Across the Eras*. Chicago: Triumph Books, 2001.

Kubek, Tony, and Terry Pluto. *Sixty-One: The Team, The Record, The Men*. New York: Macmillan Publishing Company, 1987.

Mantle, Mickey, with Herb Gluck. *The Mick*. Garden City, New York: Doubleday & Company, Inc., 1985.

Mantle, Mickey, and Phil Pepe. *My Favorite Summer 1956*. New York: Doubleday, 1991.

Pepe, Phil. *Talkin' Baseball: An Oral History of Baseball in the 1970s*. New York: Ballantine Books, 1998.

Williams, Ted, with Jim Prime. *Ted Williams' Hit List*. Toronto, Canada: Stoddart Publishing Co., 1995.

Other Sources

Baseball-Reference.com
Retrosheet.org
The New York Times
Wikipedia.com

DATE DUE

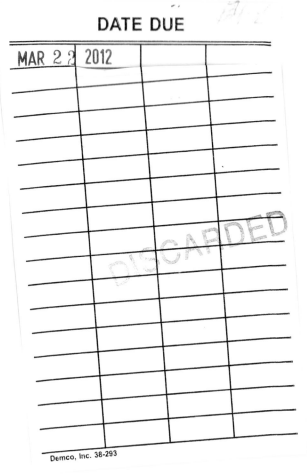

Demco, Inc. 38-293